Creating Strategic Value

JOSEPH CALANDRO JR.

CREATING STRATEGIC VALUE

Applying Value Investing Principles to Corporate Management

Columbia University Press
Publishers Since 1893
New York   Chichester, West Sussex
cup.columbia.edu
Copyright © 2020 Joseph Calandro Jr.
All rights reserved

Library of Congress Cataloging-in-Publication Data
Names: Calandro, Joseph, author.
Title: Creating strategic value : applying value investing
principles to corporate management / Joseph Calandro Jr.
Description: New York : Columbia University Press, [2020] |
Includes bibliographical references and index.
Identifiers: LCCN 2019057473 (print) | LCCN 2019057474 (ebook) |
ISBN 9780231194143 (hardback) | ISBN 9780231550673 (ebook)
Subjects: LCSH: Investment analysis. |
Corporations—Valuation. | Value investing.
Classification: LCC HG4529 .C36 2020 (print) |
LCC HG4529 (ebook) | DDC 658.15—dc23
LC record available at https://lccn.loc.gov/2019057473
LC ebook record available at https://lccn.loc.gov/2019057474

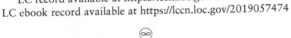

Columbia University Press books are printed on permanent
and durable acid-free paper.

Printed in the United States of America
Cover design: Noah Arlow

For Terilyn, again and always, and to the memories of
Bruce M. Bickley and Martin J. Whitman

Contents

4
Corporate Management and "Security Analysis" (including an interview with Seth A. Klarman)   51

5
Value Creating Corporate Management:
Henry E. Singleton   57

Appendix 5.1: Evaluating a Stock Buyback   69

Appendix 5.2: Managing Funding Obligations   72

6
Managerial "Rationality"   74

7
Corporate Management and "Modern Security Analysis"
(including an interview with the late Martin J. Whitman)   86

8
Value Realization Is "The Most Important Thing"   97

PREFACE TO PART 2
Practice

9
Value Realization at GEICO   109

Appendix 9.1: Note on Estimating Growth Value   129

10
Value Realization at GTI Corporation   134

Contents

Foreword

EVER SINCE BENJAMIN Graham wrote about Mr. Market's mood swings and sentimental ups and downs, astute and successful investors have practiced the art of distinguishing price from value. Graham and Dodd advised investors in their seminal book *Security Analysis* that a financial asset should be purchased when its market price is significantly below its intrinsic value. This celebrated principle, known as the margin of safety, has guided the investment decisions of many value investors in the past and will continue to do so for many years to come. But financial assets are not the only assets where this principle is applicable. Indeed, many strategic decisions in corporate finance, from takeovers to corporate risk management, can benefit from the insights that one finds in *Security Analysis* and *The Intelligent Investor*. Surprisingly, very few books document these corporate finance applications in a comprehensive manner, with the exception of Joseph Calandro's *Applied Value Investing*, which covered several specific applications. His new book, *Creating Strategic Value*, more comprehensively illustrates the application of value investing principles in many areas of corporate management, ranging from the use of excess cash to stock buybacks and acquisitions.

Value investing and its underlying principles can influence corporate management in two separate ways or channels. On the one hand, value investors are active investors, and there are many examples of how they can influence the management of corporations. This channel is more frequently discussed. For example, Benjamin Graham himself knew the importance of shareholder activism (beautifully illustrated by Jeff Gramm in *Dear Chairman*), and Mario Gabelli's analysts at GAMCO constantly grill corporate managers on how they allocate capital within the firm. It is well known that Warren Buffett has long advocated a strategy of buying companies with a strong management team, which shows how corporate management can be a prerequisite for an effective value investing strategy. These examples illustrate how value investors, including activist investors, can guide corporate managers to create shareholder value.

But there is another channel, perhaps a road less frequently travelled, where Calandro's *Creating Strategic Value* makes a much-needed contribution. Here we ask ourselves whether and how a CEO can proactively create stakeholder value by applying the fundamental principles of value investing to how the corporation is managed and how corporate strategy is defined and implemented—and not just react to activist investors. Few authors have addressed this question until now, and Calandro shows us how successful CEOs have, and should, carry out this task.

Joseph Calandro is a skilled practitioner in the art of corporate management and corporate strategy. He has many years of experience in corporate consulting and has published his keen observations in many papers. *Creating Strategic Value* brings together much of his earlier research in one unified compendium. Calandro is also a keen observer of the changes that have taken place since Graham and Dodd first emphasized tangible assets and "net-net" stocks. Many large corporations today have huge intangible assets and many others have very large amounts of cash invested in hedge funds and private equity. This book provides useful perspectives on these changes. Yet another remarkable feature of the book is that several chapters demonstrate how famous investors such as Seth Klarman and Lee Cooperman, and famous CEOs such as Henry Singleton and Prem Watsa, have implemented the insights of value investing. There is a delightful conversation with Seth Klarman, too. The book is written in a style that allows readers with little technical knowledge of finance and business to understand the key concepts. This approach will help the book reach a larger audience.

The Gabelli Center at Fordham University is happy to say that Joseph Calandro has been a Fellow of the Center right from its inception. We can assure him that *Creating Strategic Value* will be required reading for our students and prominently displayed on our own bookshelves. We wish him the very best in his future research and publications.

Sris Chatterjee, Gabelli Chair in Global Security Analysis
Fordham University
Bronx, NY

Creating Strategic Value

Introduction

"Investment is most intelligent when it is most businesslike.
I should add that it is most successful when it is most businesslike."
—BENJAMIN GRAHAM[1]

Business students need only three well taught courses: How to
Value a Business, How to Think About Market Prices, and How
to Manage a Business.
—INSPIRED BY WARREN E. BUFFETT[2]

A GREAT DEAL HAS been written about value investing, but until fairly recently no formal attempt has been made to categorize the development of this influential school of thought over time, as far as I am aware.[3] This is important because it is difficult to forecast where a school of thought is going without first understanding where it has been. Therefore, to kick things off, I will provide my thoughts on value investing's past and present and then offer suggestions on what its future may hold.

Founding Era: 1934 to 1973

The "official" founding of value investing occurred in 1934 with the publication of Benjamin Graham and David Dodd's seminal book, *Security Analysis*. The strategic concept upon which value investing was founded is as insightful as it is simple: namely, assets purchased for less than their liquidation value (estimated as current assets less *total* liabilities or "net-net value") are a low-risk form of investment due to the "margin of safety" afforded by the discount from liquidation value. *Risk* in this context is defined as the possibility and amount of loss.

As the discipline evolved over time, some investors started estimating margins of safety off earnings power and even growth value in addition to liquidation and net asset values. In fact, scholars have classified the following three different methods of modern value investing:

- **Classic value investing,** which focuses on the balance sheet and tangible assets (sample investors include the late Max Heine and Seth Klarman);
- **Mixed value investing,** which focuses on both the balance sheet and earnings power, especially regarding replacement and private market values (sample investors include Mario Gabelli and the late Marty Whitman); and
- **Contemporary value investing,** which focuses on franchise value and the quality of corporate management to realize value over time (sample investors include Warren Buffett and Glenn Greenberg).[4]

Regardless of the approach, however, the cornerstone of professional value investing has always been, and will always remain, firmly grounded in the margin of safety principle.

The founding era effectively ends with the fourth revised edition of Benjamin Graham's immensely popular book *The Intelligent Investor*, which summarizes lessons from *Security Analysis* for a nonprofessional audience. Shortly after the edition's publication, in 1976, Graham passed away at the age of 82.

Post-Graham Era: 1973 to 1991

The start of the Post-Graham Era coincided with the great 1973–1974 bear market that, amongst other things, presented numerous investment opportunities akin to those seen at the beginning of the Founding Era. It was no coincidence that such a market environment saw the ascendancy of a number of highly successful value investors such as Gary Brinson, Jeremy Grantham, John Neff,[5] and others. During this period, modern financial economic theories began to take hold. In the book *Capital Ideas*, Peter Bernstein profiled these theories, all of which are unpopular with professional value investors:

- Economists believe that market prices are "efficient," while value investors know that, at times, market prices can behave extremely inefficiently resulting in margin of safety–rich opportunities for the patient, liquid, *and* informed investor;
- Economists believe that capital structure is "irrelevant," while value investors know that capital structure is always relevant;
- Economists believe that investments should be guided by modern portfolio theory (MPT), while value investors understand, and carefully exploit, the fact that the volatility and correlation statistics of MPT are not representative of a portfolio's risk and return profile (where *risk* is once again defined as the possibility and amount of loss); and
- Economists' option pricing models do not consider underlying value; conversely, to a professional value investor, value is a component of option pricing just like it is a pricing component of every other economic good.

Despite the success of professional value investors during this era, the challenge for Graham and Dodd's successors was to determine how the basic insights of value investing could be reinterpreted for modern investors and to demonstrate the significance of that reinterpretation given the market conditions investors were wrestling with.

Modern Era: 1991 to Present

To address this challenge, Seth Klarman, cofounder and president of The Baupost Group, picked up where Benjamin Graham left off, literally. The final chapter of Graham's *The Intelligent Investor* is titled " 'Margin of Safety' as the Central Concept of Investment," while Klarman's 1991 book is titled *Margin of Safety: Risk-Averse Value Investing Strategies for the Thoughtful Investor*. The lucidity of Klarman's book, coupled with his investing track record, helped to set the tone for the modern era of value investing.

Support for this position can be found in the influence that *Margin of Safety* has had on all prominent value investing books published after it, from Bruce Greenwald's popular book (chapter 13 profiles Klarman), to the sixth edition of *Security Analysis* (for which Klarman served as lead editor), to Howard Marks's well-regarded value investing book, *The Most Important Thing Illuminated* (which was endorsed by, and contains annotations from, Klarman).

One strength of modern value investing theory is that it can be applied to all forms of investment, not just stocks and bonds. For example, consider derivatives. Best-selling books such as *The Big Short* profiled a number of investors who really did "catch" the 2007–2008 financial crisis by purchasing credit default swaps (CDS) at margin of safety–rich prices prior to the crisis. Klarman was one of these investors.[6]

So how did these investors do it? While the specifics of their investments are not publicly available, a real-time record of similar investments exists in the influential and long-running newsletter *Grant's Interest Rate Observer*, which is published by value investor /historian/financial analyst/journalist James Grant. A compendium of his newsletters leading up to "the big short" was published in the book *Mr. Market Miscalculates*, where "Mr. Market" is Benjamin Graham's euphemism for the short-term-oriented trading environment that dominates the financial markets. Page 171 of that book, which was taken from the September 8, 2006, edition of *Grant's Interest Rate Observer*, noted that a hedge fund was "expressing a bearish view on housing in the CDS market by buying protection on the weaker tranches of at-risk mortgage structures. At the cost of $14.25 million a year, the fund has exposure to $750 million face amount of mortgage debt."

To see how margin of safety–rich this investment was at the time, consider that one way commercial insurance underwriters evaluate risk pricing is to divide the premium of risk transfer (in this case, $14.25 million) by the amount of risk (in this case, $750 million), which in this example gives a "rate on line" of $0.014. By comparison, it is common for some businesses to pay $40,000 or more per year for $1 million of general liability insurance, which equates to a "rate on line" of $0.04.

Postmodern Era

With value investing successfully being applied to so many asset classes—stocks, bonds, real estate, and derivatives—what could a postmodern era entail? One answer to this question could involve increasing applications of core value investing principles to corporate strategy and management.

Professional value investors have generally been skeptical of corporate managers. For example, in *Security Analysis*, Benjamin Graham and David Dodd observed, "It is nearly always true that the management is in the best position to judge which policies are most efficient. However, it does not follow that it will always either recognize or adopt the course most beneficial to the shareholders. It may err grievously through incompetence."[7] There have been many other examples on the same topic since.[8]

However, there have also been powerful exceptions. Consider, for example, the case of Prem Watsa, the founder, chair, and CEO of Fairfax Financial Holdings. Prior to the 2007–2008 financial crisis, he purchased economically priced CDS, which reportedly generated a gain of more than $2 billion against an investment of $341 million. While the specifics of Watsa's position are not publicly available, because he is a corporate manager, the CDS he purchased were appropriate for the balance sheet he was managing, which is to say hedging. In general, there are four ways to manage the risk of a significant balance sheet exposure: (1) reduce it, (2) diversify away from it, (3) work it down, or (4) hedge it. Each of these alternatives can be informed by value investing in general and by the margin of safety principle in particular. In the case of hedging, the results of Watsa's position speaks for itself: **Figure 0.1** profiles 10 percent or greater changes in property and casualty insurance company performance in the third quarter of 2007. The financial performance of Fairfax Financial Holdings—shown at the extreme right of the figure—is materially greater than the rest of the insurance industry at the time.

One objective of this book is to provide a theoretical foundation for a value investing–based approach to corporate strategy and management. More on this in a minute, but first we will return to the development of value investing as a school of thought.

Classifying the different eras of any school of thought is subjective, and as such frequently requires anchoring to key dates. For example, the Baroque era of music "officially" ended with the death of J. S. Bach. Maestro Bach, of course, never knew that his death would end an era any more than Benjamin Graham could have known that some future author would date the close of the founding era of value investing with the 1973 edition of *The*

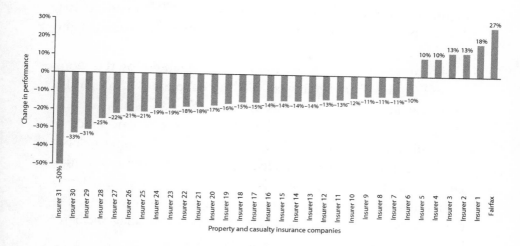

FIGURE 0.1 Margin of Safety–based Hedging. *Data source*: Dowling & Partners, *IBNR Weekly* #39, October 5, 2007, 8. The names of the other thirty-one insurers are available from Dowling. I changed the order of the names. We will return to this figure in the **Conclusion** of this book.

Intelligent Investor. Nevertheless, such classifications are useful for both practitioners and researchers, especially when contemplating what the future may hold.

Whether value investing influences and helps define corporate strategy and management in the future or not, investors and corporate managers alike can only benefit from studying the lessons of Graham and his followers. Professional value investing has been applied across a variety of asset classes and market environments and, when applied skillfully, has generated exceptional returns at relatively low levels of risk. To facilitate an understanding of how this school of thought could be practically applied to corporate management, this book is structured in two parts.

Part 1 establishes a theoretical foundation for value investing and corporate management, which is important because, first, value investing texts pertain to investing, not to corporate management. Building off this foundation, **Part 2** brings the theory to life via historical case studies of value realization in action. The chapters in this part of the book are somewhat technical and should be approached as such.

Similar to my first book, most of the chapters of this book (including this **Introduction** as well as chapters 2 through 11, inclusive) are based on published research papers that I have rewritten for this book. I publish papers on the practical side of the academic literature and have found it a useful outlet to both develop and disseminate my ideas. By collecting and rewriting a number of these papers for this book, I hope to reach a larger audience and advance the continued study of value investing, particularly as it applies to corporate strategy and management for both practicing executives and researchers alike.

APPENDIX

Common Ground and/or Areas of Further Research

> "Modern academic research has moved the theory of financial
> market behavior in the direction of Graham and Dodd."
> —BRUCE GREENWALD[1]

IS THERE *ANY* COMMON ground between academic finance and professional value investing? There certainly can be, as I have experienced at certain times in my career as a corporate advisor, researcher, and professor. More importantly, however, simply asking the question can point to areas of potential further research that could prove insightful both academically and practically. This appendix profiles some of my thoughts on this topic.

We begin with the **efficient market hypothesis**. Few people would argue with the thought that, for the most part, financial markets do seem to "get it right" most of the time. Financial markets do not get it right all of the time because the people who make up the markets do not, and never will, act 100 percent "efficiently." Therefore, a method of understanding the causes, drivers, and consequences of abnormally volatile market behavior (i.e., inefficiency), beyond the psychological considerations of behavioral economics, would likely be welcome by many professional value investors.

Consider, for example, the actions of governments in financial markets across history. From Alexander Hamilton assuming the Revolutionary War debt of the states at 100 cents on the dollar[2] and

Andrew Carnegie's adroit exploitation of the 1870 tariff[3] to Warren Buffett's "bet" that the government would not let firms like GE and Goldman Sachs "fail" during the 2007–2008 financial crisis,[4] and to the current monetary policies that have resulted in more than $10 trillion of fixed income securities yielding *negative* rates,[5] governments have had a tremendous impact on financial market behavior. Formal financial research into this phenomenon—meaning, the extent to which abnormally volatile market behavior, to the downside *and* upside, traces back to some form of governmental action or policy—would be of immense practical interest.

Moving on to **modern portfolio theory (MPT) and asset pricing factor models**, which employ volatility as a proxy for risk. However, volatility is *not* risk; in fact, at times, the most volatile securities can have the least risk of loss. "For example, the debt of Enron, perhaps the most stigmatized company after an accounting scandal forced it into bankruptcy in 2001, traded as low as 10 cents on the dollar of claim; ultimate recoveries are expected to be six times that amount."[6] Because of many similar examples,[7] some investors use these models as contra-indicators. However, this use does not mean that the volatility and correlation statistics of MPT and asset pricing factor models are without strategic value.

For example, select professional value investors may be interested in managing institutional money. Institutional asset allocation strategies are very different from professional value investing strategies; in fact, institutions often buy/sell when professional value investors are selling/buying. As such, professional value investing strategies should not be correlated to institutional asset allocation strategies, which can be quantified in the MPT–based analyses that many institutions employ. Not coincidentally, **Chapter 1** profiles an example of this.

Much the same can be said of factor models. When you get away from the incorrect claim that such models measure "risk" and instead focus on the insights that can be generated into

10

required rates of return for capital allocation purposes within a firm, useful findings can emerge. For example, I created a two-factor model for property and casualty insurance companies that has been successfully used at both the enterprise and business unit levels.[8] In short, MPT and factor models can augment more traditional forms of value investing analyses; therefore, in my opinion, they should generally not be dismissed out of hand.

My least favorite modern financial theory is the proposition that **capital structure is irrelevant.** I have repeatedly seen capital structure become the most relevant strategic consideration within a firm; however, when you look at the broad economy over time it can be hard to argue with the irrelevance proposition. Consider, for example, the history of commercial and industrial loans since the year 1981, Ronald Reagan's first year as president (figure 0.2).[9]

Long-term macro trends aside, we know that there is a "credit cycle" and that some debt-heavy capital structures will fail when the cycle turns down. No one knows exactly which capital structures are going to fail, or when, but that does not mean exposure to such structures cannot be assessed and managed. Greater

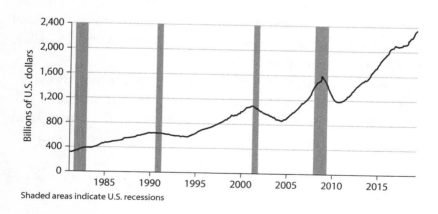

Shaded areas indicate U.S. recessions

FIGURE 0.2 Commercial and Industrial Loans from January 1, 1981, to April 1, 2019. *Source*: Fred Economic Data, https://fred.stlouisfed.org/series/BUSLOANS (accessed May 16, 2019).

academic insight into this phenomenon—identifying when capital structure in general becomes *very* relevant—would be incredibly valuable. Consider the modern (as of mid-2019) example of "private middle-market loans," which Jim Grant describes as follows:

> The private middle market loan is a kind of do-it-yourself product; having extended a credit, also to a speculative-grade business, institutional investors retain it on their own balance sheets. They thus bypass the banks, which, for the most part, have been happy to be bypassed, the burgeoning demand for deal-related credit notwithstanding. The middle market is illiquid and opaque.[10]

Despite the illiquidity and opaqueness—or, perhaps, because of them—this market has grown powerfully to approximately $800 million.[11] Following the interest rate repression that occurred across the globe in the wake of the 2007–2008 financial crisis, many institutions undertook a "hunt for yield" that led them into similar markets.

I recently spoke with a CFO about his firm's exposure to this market, and specifically how to begin thinking about the accumulated risks of a private middle market loans portfolio. I immediately referred him to the Altman Z-score, a time-tested financial distress model for both publicly and privately held firms, which is profiled in **Chapter 10** of this book.

About a week later, the CFO called and told me that his money manager indicated that they do not have the information to calculate Z-scores.[12] Now, as you can see below, the information needed to calculate a private company Z-score is very basic:

$$\text{Z-score for privately held firms} = 6.56X_1 + 3.26X_2 + 6.72X_3 + 1.05X_4$$

where
X_1 = working capital / total assets

X_2 = retained earnings / total assets
X_3 = earnings before interest and taxes / total assets
X_4 = net worth / total liabilities

The following criteria are used to interpret this model:

- **Safe Zone** = $Z > 2.60$,
- **Distress Zone** = $Z < 1.10$, and
- **Grey Zone** = $1.10 \leq Z \leq 2.60$.

I therefore advised this CFO to begin investigating hedging opportunities for his portfolio and to find another money manager as quickly as possible.[13] Understanding how dynamics like this fit into the pattern of past credit crises and/or as an input into some kind of systemic credit risk model (that is *not* VaR or VaR-related) would be both insightful academically and of immediate practical use (assuming another financial crisis does not occur before the publication of this book).[14]

We turn now to **derivatives and option pricing models.** In many ways, each of the four core theories of academic finance is cumulative: if you believe that financial markets are efficient, it is not a stretch to believe that capital structure is irrelevant and that volatility is a valid measure of risk. However, when these things are simultaneously shown not to be true it can result in extremely nonlinear market behavior, which options and derivatives pricing models vastly underestimate. To the knowledgeable market participant, such dynamics can present lucrative investment opportunities. However, as there is no formal theory that explains such opportunities, few people are able to see the opportunities for what they are prior to volatility drastically expanding. This was the theme of Michael Lewis's best-selling book on the 2007–2008 financial crisis, *The Big Short.*[15]

As another example, consider the pre–Big Short economy. At the time, I was advising a CFO on his risk accumulations and in the process noticed a large exposure to Berkshire Hathaway. Long-dated Berkshire CDS were then trading around 10 basis points. I therefore advised this CFO to buy as much of this CDS as he could, which he promptly rejected: "There is absolutely **NO** way that Berkshire Hathaway is going to go bankrupt!" He was, of course, entirely correct, but when it comes to derivatives pricing his comment was also completely irrelevant. To make a long story short, in both 2008 and 2009 the same CDS traded over 400 basis points (and nearly as high as 500 basis points).

Nassim Nicholas Taleb has taken advantage of similar opportunities as a trader, and he has written eloquently about them in books such as *Fooled by Randomness, The Black Swan, Antifragile,* and several others. Some professional value investors, including Prem Watsa as discussed in the **Introduction**, have taken advantage of mispriced derivatives from time to time, and I sometimes advise corporate managers on the same topic, as profiled in **Chapter 1**, which is a *very* ripe area for academic research.

PART 1
Theory

CHAPTER 1 PROFILES MY thoughts on how to apply a value investing approach to corporate management. In the book's first draft, it served as the **Conclusion**, but a number of reviewers strongly suggested that the book should lead with this material rather than end with it. On reflection, I agreed, as it sets the tone for, and puts into context, all of the material that follows.

In practice, I have found it helpful to talk about value investing principles to corporate managers in the context of an existing business problem, rather than to simply lead off with it. For example, in the case of an acquisition where an acquirer is paying a significant control premium, I mention the margin of safety principle and how successful value investors employ it in a way that can facilitate corporate strategy, which is the subject of **Chapter 2**.

In other discussions, I speak about the role of cash in corporate strategy, explaining how certain professional value investors employ cash as a competitive advantage, which is often contrary to how many corporate managers think about either cash or competitive advantage, which is the subject of **Chapter 3.**

Some corporate managers are obviously familiar with Graham and Dodd's seminal work, *Security Analysis*, and some are even familiar with successful value investors beyond Warren Buffett. When I talk to such managers, I cover a broad variety of topics including how *Security Analysis* can apply to corporate management in general and, if applicable, I reference an interview I conducted with Seth Klarman—the lead editor of the sixth edition of *Security* Analysis—on this topic, which is included in **Chapter 4.**

Many corporate managers are interested in a specific example of someone who actually "did it"—meaning, successfully applied value investing principles to corporate management—and what specifically was accomplished. I often begin my reply to such inquiries with the example of the late Henry Singleton of Teledyne, who is profiled in **Chapter 5.**

Behavioral economics is very popular these days, and while it is a relatively new academic discipline, value investors have for years focused on "rationality" as a key indicator of resource allocation skill. Therefore, a study of rationality revealed a number of practical insights, which can be widely leveraged by both corporate and investment managers, as profiled in **Chapter 6.**

It is generally recognized that the scope of corporate skill sets is changing and evolving beyond operations to include greater levels of investment and financial acumen. The late Martin J. Whitman was at the forefront of this evolution, and as such, I have applied his work to corporate management, which includes an interview I conducted with him on this topic a few years before he passed away (**Chapter 7**).

Capabilities are important, but corporate success is defined when value, broadly defined, is realized. In fact, it can be argued that value realization is "The Most Important Thing," as discussed in **Chapter 8**, which is the final chapter of **Part 1.**

16

A word on structure to conclude this **Preface**. A number of the chapters (specifically, 2, 4, 5, 7, and 8) are based on influential value investing works from which I have drawn corporate management lessons. The reason for this, as previously noted, is that most of the material on value investing pertains to investing, not corporate management. This, of course, does not mean that these works are without managerial value. After all, professional value investors such as Warren Buffett, Mario Gabelli, Paul Singer, and Mitch Julis have all founded and led (and still lead) successful businesses. However, by explicitly drawing managerial lessons from influential value investing texts, I am able to make a direct connection from this school of thought to corporate management. This link is important for a number of reasons, including the fact that many corporate managers have never been trained in, nor exposed to, professional value investing, and this linkage can help facilitate such training.

Lastly, a word about the value investing works I chose to draw on in these chapters. I chose titles that: (1) were authored by successful professional value investors, (2) I felt were seminal, (3) the authors agreed to speak with me, and (4) my findings were significant enough to be published in a practitioner-oriented research journal. These rules necessarily limited the universe of works I was able to reference. Hopefully, my selection process resulted in findings that both current and future corporate managers and researchers alike will find useful.

1

Value Investing and Corporate Management

Overview

"True investors can exploit the recurrent excessive optimism and
excessive apprehension of the speculative public."
—BENJAMIN GRAHAM[1]

"Will management *itself* follow the Graham and Dodd principles
in investing the shareholders' money?"
—GLENN GREENBERG (ITALICS ORIGINAL)[2]

GREENBERG'S QUOTE ABOVE does not mean that corporate managers should attempt to become professional value investors. Value investing represents a very small portion of the money management universe, and only a very small portion of that already very small portion represents successful professional value investors. Further, corporate managers tend to be trained in, and skilled at, strategy and operations, not investment. There are, of course, exceptions such as media executive John Malone, Prem Watsa of Fairfax Financial Holdings, and the Tisch family of Loews, etc., but they are exceptions. Nevertheless, there are several practical ways that corporate managers can "follow the Graham and Dodd principles in investing the shareholders' money."

First, consider firms with regulated balance sheets. Institutional asset allocation strategies are often employed to invest the funds recorded on these balance sheets. Such strategies tend to be cyclical: investment returns rise and fall in tandem with "the market."

19

As such, firms that employ these strategies also employ value-at-risk (VaR) models and related processes to inform their portfolio management activities. Because value investing is inherently contrarian,[3] it tends to be countercyclical to institutional strategies: when institutional allocators are buying, value investors tend to be selling and vice versa. As such, professional value investing strategies should generally decrease institutional VaRs while increasing institutional portfolio returns.

Some context before we go on: I do not like either institutional asset allocation strategies or VaR. If I were managing a firm, I would limit my use of each to the utmost, but I am not managing a firm; rather, I advise managers of firms and, for a variety of reasons, these managers use VaR in the management of their institutional asset allocation–derived portfolios. Therefore, to have an impact, one sometimes has to operate within an institutional framework. Some of the firms I advise are strongly capitalized. I have shown such firms that, even with a small allocation to a professional, top-tier value investing fund, their institutionally managed portfolios would have, at the time of analyses, simultaneously *increased* the portfolios' returns while *decreasing* their VaRs.

Figure 1.1 profiles the impact of two different value investing funds on financial institutions' investment portfolios (the example has been scrubbed for presentation purposes). As can be seen, both funds have a dramatic impact on overall portfolio performance even though the measurements were taken during periods of low market volatility (in 2017). Further, and as noted above, professional value investing strategies tend to be countercyclical and therefore the funds' performance should be even better during periods when volatility spikes and markets are in distress.[4] However, despite the compelling nature of exhibits like this one, few corporate managers have taken advantage of such opportunities. Questions I am asked go something like this:

Question: If professional value investing is so good, why isn't everyone doing it?

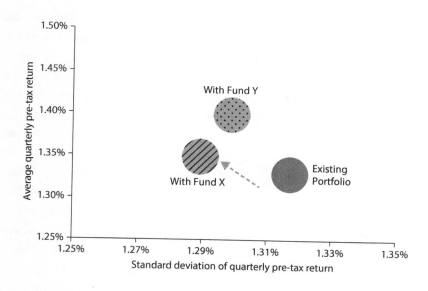

	Porfolio Size	1-in-250 VaR	1-in-500 VaR
Existing Portfolio		−$168M	−$178M
With Fund X	$13.2B	−$165M	−$175M
With Fund Y		−$164M	−$175M

FIGURE 1.1 Volatility (*not* risk) versus Return of an Institutional Investment Portfolio. *Note*: The names of both of the firms and the funds have been withheld, and actual portfolio dollars and percentages have been scrubbed for illustration purposes. Shaded cells in the table reflect existing portfolio VaRs at each return period or level of confidence.

Answer: The reason why an opportunity like this exists is that very few corporate managers are even looking at it, let alone doing it.

Question: That doesn't make sense. Why aren't they looking at it? Somebody should have noticed it by now.

Answer: Firms like Berkshire Hathaway, Fairfax, Loews, and Markel are investing this way, and have been for some time, as the executives at each firm have repeatedly indicated. As for broader adoption, why didn't professional baseball managers employ sabermetrics before the experiences of the Oakland A's, as chronicled in the book *Moneyball*, made it popular? People tend to stick with things they are familiar with, and corporate management as a group is not familiar with how professional value investing can be employed in an institutional asset allocation setting, and neither are the investment consultants nor the investment bankers who advise them. So, opportunities like this exist because people are either not looking at them or are ignoring them.

For another example, consider corporate risk management. Following the financial crisis of 2007–2008, many firms spent a great deal of time and effort developing and building up their risk management functions. Such functions tend to be focused on compliance, regulatory, and internal reporting, which can have a performance downside. For instance, and as noted above, firms that employ institutional asset allocation strategies are at risk of loss when cycles take a downturn and/or when markets become volatile. This fact is well known, yet relatively few executives actively manage it. For example, in mid- to late 2017, I spoke with a number of corporate managers whose institutional portfolios had significant equity and equity-like allocations. At the time (May 26, 2017), the volatility index (VIX) traded at the following prices: Open \$12.29, High \$12.52, **Low \$9.65**, and **Close \$9.81**.[5]

I advised the corporate managers I spoke with to look seriously at the VIX, even if only from a relatively minor allocation perspective, given their exposures and the nonlinear nature of derivative payoffs. However, few corporate managers—in consultation with their investment consultants and investment bankers— took advantage of the opportunity prior to early February 2018, which was when volatility hit the equity markets. For example, on February 9, 2018, the VIX traded at the following prices: Open \$18.44, **High \$50.30**, Low \$16.80, and **Close \$29.06**.[6]

Several weeks later, I received a number of follow-up phone calls, which went something like this:

Question: Hey, great call on the VIX, but how did you know volatility was going to spike like that within the year?

Answer: Thanks, but all I did was notice how low equity risk pricing was, and then I presented that fact to clients with relatively large equity/equity-like exposures. Regarding timing, I did not know when volatility was going to hit the equity market, but you do not have to know that. If you have a large exposure and someone quotes you a very low price to insure or hedge it, why wouldn't you take advantage of it? It's like living in a well-known hurricane zone, and an insurance company quotes you a very low price to insure your house: wouldn't you insure it? You *cannot* know when a bad storm is going to hit, but you do know that one *can* hit, and you have a large asset to protect so. . . . [7] The same logic applies across markets. [8]

Regardless of examples like these, a core premise of this book is that value investing principles can be applied not only to corporate investing, but also to corporate strategy and management. Before explaining how, we will first outline several considerations for applying a value investing approach to corporate management. First, though, a disclaimer: what follows is my opinion and my opinion *only*. Further, what follows is a general framework, *not* a research hypothesis to be "accepted" or "rejected." Not everyone will agree with me; in fact, if I am doing my job right, many people will disagree with me. Regardless, the information below should be kept in mind while reading the following chapters, all of which I hope prove useful.

The first consideration is to derive a unique customer value proposition *and* to determine how the margin of safety principle will facilitate that proposition over time. As an example, consider that Warren Buffett has people literally lining up to sell him a dollar of their assets for pennies on the dollar, and—and!—they actually get applauded for doing so instead of getting called before a regulator, sued, or otherwise hauled off to the back of the prover-bial woodshed. This amazing achievement, in my opinion, ranks him—along with the late John D. Rockefeller—as the preeminent strategist across American business history.[9],[10]

There are, of course, other albeit less dramatic examples that can be cited here, but *you* have to determine how to apply the margin of safety principle in your business and in your own way, which is a great deal harder than it may first appear. It is *far* easier to buy what everyone else is buying, at prices everyone else is pay-ing, than to take a contrarian point of view and buy when every-one else is selling.

The second consideration is how to make decisions about busi-ness activity financing. Pick the right investors and creditors, and they can powerfully enable strategic execution over time. Pick incorrectly, however, and not only could your results suffer, but the process might make you miserable. Here are a few historical examples:

- Thomas Edison and George Westinghouse are two of the most creative entrepreneurs in history, and yet each lost control of companies they founded for financial reasons;
- Jay Gould sold his stake in the Union Pacific Railroad, which he had successfully turned around, because he could not resolve the "financial albatross" of governmental debt (see **Chapter 11** for more information); and
- Steve Jobs lost control of Apple, to which he later trium-phantly returned, after being voted out by his own board of directors.

In short, funding and capital structure are paramount, second only to strategy, which was the first consideration mentioned above. One professional value investor explained his views to me this way: we generally look for companies that optimize opera-tional leverage, which is "good leverage," and that tend to stay away from financial leverage, which is "bad leverage." When we see firms with low operational leverage and high financial leverage, we watch them, because it is usually just a matter of time before they go into distress, which can present opportunities.

Again, this is a general framework only. There are cases—John Malone prominent amongst them—of corporate managers who employ debt in a manner that facilitates rather than constrains long-term results, but they are specialty cases and therefore you had better be a specialist to deploy them. If you are not, limit the amount of debt you use, if you use it at all. Instead, focus on accumulating cash balances when "times are good" so that the cash can be deployed when prices are favorable (such as "when times are bad").[11]

The third consideration is "balance," broadly defined. Increasingly, corporate management encompasses not only operational skills but also greater levels of investment and financial skills. Balancing all three of these skills—all of the time—is not easy, and has been successfully accomplished only rarely over time.

An enabler of this kind of integrated skill set is a balanced focus on current market cycles as well countercyclical considerations. Information on current market cycles can be found in conventional sources while countercyclical information is often found in alternative sources. For example, the **Introduction** profiled the position that Prem Watsa of Fairfax Financial Holdings took prior to the infamous "big short." I learned of such opportunities in the pages of *Grant's Interest Rate Observer*, which is also where I learned of the underpriced VIX opportunity from earlier in this chapter. *Grant's* is a leading value investing-based periodical, but it is much less popular with corporate managers, as is Marc Faber's equally influential *Gloom, Boom & Doom Report*. I recommend, at a minimum, that you read both.

Alternative information can also come in quantitative form. The quintessential example is the use of sabermetrics in professional baseball as profiled in Michael Lewis's book *Moneyball*, but we will profile another example in **Chapter 10** of this book via the successful use of a financial distress model in a turnaround management context. Needless to say, models should only be used if they are clearly and thoroughly understood by *all* who use them: analysts and corporate managers alike.

Balance is also required in how corporate managers choose to spend their time, which is extremely important and often misunderstood. For example, in 2012, journalist Tom Ricks wrote a thought-provoking book titled *The Generals: American Military Command from World War II to Today*, which forcefully posited a decline in U.S. generalship from World War II to the present day. I viewed a speech Ricks gave at Berkeley on *YouTube* where he spoke of the former commander of the Iraq War, Lt. General Ricardo Sánchez, and how the general actually disciplined a subordinate for misstating the number of tires in a combat zone ("Yesterday you said your battalion was short twenty-four tires, today you said twenty-two! Did you find two tires?!") Ricks correctly observed that discrepancies like this are not the type of thing you want a commanding general spending time on, and I am fairly certain that most of the people reading this book would agree with that assessment even though many corporate managers effectively do the same thing all of the time.

Management in general has three broad categories: the first pertains to current product and service offerings, and the operations to produce those products/services. This category takes up a preponderance of managerial time and attention, and it is often referred to as business as usual (BaU). Absent any kind of innovation or disruption, the most efficient corporate managers in BaU earn the highest returns. Taken to extremes, however, a focus on efficiency can devolve into endless meetings, second-guessing and micromanagement. Because activity is a measure of efficiency—notice I did not say it was *the* measure of efficiency—corporate managers often strive to fill their day, and the easiest way to fill one's day is to micromanage subordinates. There is an epidemic of micromanagement today accompanied by a corresponding dearth of strategic thinking.

One benefit of a value investing approach to corporate management is the recognition that while most of one's professional life will be spent in BaU, opportunities arise during periods of disruption—in other words, in the "thick tails" of real-life probability distributions. At such times, prices can become volatile, resulting in margin of safety–rich assets or liabilities that will be either overlooked or ignored by others. As a result, while the value investing corporate manager will focus on BaU, they will not be consumed by it.

The battle in the short term is frequently won or lost in BaU, but the war over the long term is won in "the tails" by economically mitigating the risk of "black swan" losses while capitalizing on disruptively innovative opportunities, which are the second and third managerial categories.[12] While this strategy may sound simple, I assure you it is not, which is why so few people are able to do it.[13]

BaU has a certain bureaucratic logic and organizational momentum to it that, frankly, employees ignore at their peril. For example, if your firm does not take a contrarian view, buys when and what everyone else is buying, and ignores the potential for extreme events in the thick tails of real-life probability distributions, you will be expected to do the same—as efficiently as possible, of course, or you will likely have to find another job. This is possibly a reason why so many successful value investors founded their own firms and why only one of the corporate managers profiled in this book worked their way up to the corner office: Tony Nicely of GEICO. All of the others either started their own firms or were called in at the corporate level: Henry Singleton was passed over for the top job at Litton Industries, which caused him to start Teledyne, James La Fleur was on GTI's board prior to his appointment as CEO, Jay Gould gained control of the Union Pacific Railroad as an investor, Warren Buffett acquired Berkshire Hathaway and then transformed it into what it is today, Prem Watsa founded Fairfax, Mario Gabelli founded Gamco Investors, and Mitch Julis and Josh Friedman founded Canyon Capital Advisors.

Therefore, contrary to so many other strategy and management books, this book is *not* a popular "how to" that promises success and riches on the happy way up the corporate ladder. Implementing the approach profiled here *will* be an uphill battle, which may cause many of you to either start your own firms or look for alternative ways to implement the approach. Either way, however, the journey will not be easy, but it will be worth it: for yourselves, your customers/clients, your employees, and your investors/creditors.

The fourth consideration is clarity, and to explain what this means I will refer to one of my favorite books, *The Art of War* by Sun Tzu.[14] It is reported that Sun Tzu once advised a local monarch on military strategy. The monarch challenged him to turn his bevy of concubines into an effective army and Sun Tzu agreed. For the commanders, Sun Tzu chose the monarch's two favorite concubines. After specifically telling them what he wanted done, Sun Tzu called formation and gave an order. Instead of obeying, the concubines giggled. Sun Tzu once again explained what he wanted done and asked if there were any questions. As there were none, he once again called formation and gave an order. However, instead of obeying, the concubines once again giggled.

Sun Tzu replied that when a general's orders are not followed, he must first look back to the orders that were given. If the orders were not clear, nonperformance is the general's fault. However, in this case, Sun Tzu twice provided very specific and very clear orders, but they were not followed. If orders are very clear, but are still not executed, the fault lies with the subordinate commanders. As a result, he had the two commanding concubines beheaded. He then appointed two new commanders, called formation, and gave an order, which was immediately obeyed.

When most people hear this story for the first time, they understandably focus on the beheadings, but first consider Sun Tzu's thoughts on providing clear instructions. Frankly, across society today, clear speaking and writing are very much dying arts. Perhaps as a result, many corporate managers' instructions can be somewhat opaque. Maybe such managers do not know what they want done, which is why their communications are unclear; if so, it would be far better to have a subordinate prepare options that can be evaluated rather than having them spin their wheels while a solution is being "iterated." Significantly, this suggestion applies to new hires as well as existing employees. For example, the first two concubines obviously had no idea what was in store for them. Had they been clearly apprised of their duties as commanders, and of the consequences of nonperformance, things might have turned out differently for them.

In sum, corporate managerial clarity benefits employees, customers, regulators, owners, and creditors, especially when the actions undertaken reconcile to the words that are spoken over time—in other words, when corporate management behavior is "rational," as we will see in **Chapter 6.**

I find that behavior tends to be irrational when people are arrogant; therefore, our fifth managerial consideration is humility.[15] In an interview following the publication of *Ike's Bluff: President Eisenhower's Secret Battle to Save the World,* author Evan Thomas noted how impressed he was by successful people like Dwight Eisenhower, who are so confident in their abilities "that they can afford to be humble." As you may know, President Eisenhower's skills were widely discounted by the scholars of his day, but historical research is increasingly pointing out how such assessments were completely wrong.[16] Regardless, I do not think Eisenhower gets enough credit for all he accomplished, especially from a financial perspective. For example, he was the last fiscally disciplined president of the United States, so much so that there is not even a close second even though his term of office ended in 1961.[17]

Eisenhower did not just become humble once he was elected president; he generally acted that way throughout his life.[18] As did

Jay Gould, as we will see in **Chapter 11**, which may come as a surprise to many people given all of the negative things written about him over the years. Similarly, perhaps the best example Warren Buffett has set is that someone can be both successful and a multibillionaire while remaining humble. Along this line, the professional value investors I know are also humble, which is interesting when you compare them to all of the arrogance in the world today: in institutional investing/Wall Street, corporate America, education, the court jesters of the media and, of course, the politics of both parties.[19] Perhaps as a result, a number of these investors told me that their firms operate under strict "no asshole rules," referencing the incredibly good book by Professor Robert Sutton, *The No Asshole Rule: Building a Civilized Workplace and Surviving One That Isn't.*

To be blunt, the days of "the imperial CEO," when the corporate manager was "the smartest guy in the room"—whether he actually was or not—should be over. Today's markets are difficult,

Table 1.1
Value Investing Corporate Management Considerations

---

1. Unique value proposition *and* how the margin of safety will enable that proposition
2. How will business activities be funded or financed?
3. Balance:
   a) across operations, finance, and investment
   b) of cyclical and counter-cyclical dynamics as reflected in mainstream *and* alternative information sources
   c) between business-as-usual processes *and* the "thick tails" of nonlinear events to both the upside *and* downside
4. Clarity of communication *and* transparency of expectations
5. Humility
6. Produce results that compound over time

---

and they will likely become increasingly more difficult over time. Therefore, it will become increasingly harder to run a successful business.[20] Why make it more difficult by being an asshole? Today's society is badly in need of a healthy dose of humility, and there is no reason why successful corporate (and investment) managers cannot be at the forefront of it.[21]

Our sixth and final consideration is the production of long-term results that maximize compounding, which is *the* way to wealth. Value investors know this, and they know how to facilitate it; in other words, they will produce results that compound. And they know how to manage the people who work for them to facilitate this over time.

2

Corporate Strategy and the "Margin of Safety"

"The asset value, the earning power of the company, the financial position as compared with other companies in the same industry, the trend of earnings, and the ability of the management to meet constantly changing conditions—all of these factors have an important bearing on the value of the company's securities."
—BENJAMIN GRAHAM AND SPENCER MEREDITH[1]

"Good businesses are generally considered those with strong barriers to entry, limited capital requirements, reliable customers, low risk technological obsolescence, abundant growth possibilities, and thus significant and growing free cash flow."
—SETH A. KLARMAN[2]

AS NOTED PREVIOUSLY, the margin of safety principle—investing in assets or projects only when the price or cost of doing so is appreciably less than conservatively estimated values—is something that *all* value investors adhere to. Indeed, Warren Buffett stated that Berkshire Hathaway insists "on a margin of safety in our purchase price. If we calculate the value of a common stock to be only slightly higher than its price, we are not interested in buying. We believe this margin of safety principle, so strongly emphasized by Benjamin Graham, to be the cornerstone of investment success."[3] Seth Klarman discusses the mechanics of the margin of safety in his book on the subject:

By always buying at a significant discount to underlying business value and giving preference to tangible assets over intangibles.

(This does not mean that there are not excellent investment opportunities in businesses with valuable intangible assets.) By replacing current holdings as better bargains come along. By selling when the market price of any investment comes to reflect its underlying value and by holding cash, if necessary, until other attractive investments become available.[4]

Some may read this quote as solely pertaining to money management. However, corporate strategy often precipitates corporate investment, and therefore this chapter will analyze this quote phrase by phrase in a corporate strategy context. Doing so will help demonstrate the applicability of the margin of safety principle to corporate strategy and thereby help lay the foundation for the rest of the book.

Buying at a Significant Discount to Underlying Business Value

As the margin of safety principle pertains to discount pricing, it reconciles with the "low cost" foundation of corporate strategy.[5] Yet, many corporate managers undertake a variety of initiatives at high prices. For example, in the first quarter of 2011, corporate managers "paid the most for takeovers since before the collapse of Lehman Brothers Holdings, Inc."[6] With regard to Lehman, prior to its historic failure, it engaged in numerous acquisitions "at the top of the market," thereby paying premium prices, as many other firms have done. Contrast this behavior with the acquisition track record of Berkshire Hathaway that, as noted above, operates in accordance with the margin of safety principle.

Lehman Brothers also bought back shares of its stock at very high prices[7]—so high, in fact, that some Lehman employees felt the firm should have been selling its stock rather than buying it!

Economical buying also pertains to hedging and risk management. For example, many modern financial models include a volatility component, so when volatility is low financial instruments can be priced very cheaply.[8] Hedging at such times can be *very* economical; and yet, as we saw in the **Introduction**, corporate managers rarely exploit this form of strategic opportunity. Perhaps they focus on short-term performance targets rather than on longer-term results.[9] Whatever the reason, many corporate managers seem to hedge only after volatility, and thus pricing spikes.[10]

In contrast, consider how Klarman "buys put options and credit-default swaps, which he calls 'cheap insurance,' to protect Baupost [his investment firm] against risks such as a steep fall in the stock market or a surge in inflation. . . . In an October 2008 letter to shareholders, the firm said it benefited from credit-default swaps, without saying what the swaps were meant to protect against."[11] According to journalist Michael Lewis, Klarman was one of the few investors who purchased favorably priced credit default swaps during the boom that preceded the 2007–2008 financial crisis.[12]

Giving Preference to Tangible Assets

Applied to corporate strategy, "giving preference to tangible assets" can be restated as "protect and manage your balance sheet," which stands in contrast to the financial economic theory that capital structure is "irrelevant."[13] As all financial crises—including the one that occurred in 2007–2008—demonstrate, capital structure and balance sheet management are extremely relevant. For example, before it failed before 2008, Lehman Brothers's debt-to-equity ratio was a staggering forty-four to one.[14] Even worse, during the boom that preceded the crisis, some financial executives did not even know their firms' balance sheets. For example, one of the investors profiled in *The Big Short* would "go to meetings with Wall Street CEOs and ask them the most basic questions about their balance sheets. 'They didn't know,' he said. 'They didn't know their own balance sheets.'"[15]

Conversely, balance sheet analysis has been a core value investing capability since the discipline's founding. According to Bruce Greenwald, "The special importance that Graham and Dodd placed on balance sheet valuations remains one of their most important contributions to the idea of what constitutes a 'thorough' analysis of intrinsic value."[16] To understand why, consider the following extended quote from *Margin of Safety*:

> Historically investors have found attractive opportunities in companies with substantial *"hidden assets,"* such as an overfunded pension fund, real estate carried on the balance sheet below market value, or a profitable finance subsidiary that could be sold at a significant gain. Amidst a broad–based decline in business and asset values, however, some hidden assets become less valuable and in some cases may become *hidden liabilities.* A decline in the stock market will reduce the value of pension fund assets; previously overfunded plans may become underfunded. Real estate, carried on companies' balance sheets at historical cost, may no longer be undervalued. . . .[17] (italics added)

Executives who actively manage their balance sheets can move to efficiently close "value gaps" created by hidden assets[18] or mitigate the potential value destruction of hidden liabilities through proactive strategic risk management initiatives[19] and shareholder communications.[20]

There Are Opportunities in Businesses with Valuable Intangible Assets

Intangible assets create value to the extent they enable a *franchise*, which is value investing nomenclature for a firm operating with a sustainable competitive advantage. The concept of competitive advantage is the foundation of modern corporate strategy;

however, it can be very difficult to value given its obviously intangible nature and indefinite life span.[21] Nevertheless, firms that are able to create and sustain a competitive advantage can present lucrative acquisition opportunities *if* they are available at a reasonable margin of safety. The classic value investing example is Warren Buffett's 1995 acquisition of GEICO, which realized significant value as both a margin of safety–rich acquisition and as a long-term growth business (**Chapter 9**).

Replacing Current Holdings as Better Bargains Come Along

According to the late strategist Bruce Henderson, "Although there is a real question whether most companies have an adequate control over the deployment of their financial resources, redeployment of financial resources is the cornerstone of all business strategy."[22] There are various ways to address resource redeployment (or resource conversion), only two of which will be profiled here. The first involves the distribution of a significant portion of a firm's equity to shareholders by way of special dividend, which is replaced with debt. This form of capital redeployment forces the kind of performance dynamics and pressures commonly found in a leveraged buyout. For example, Sealed Air Corporation redeployed its capital in this manner in 1989 with the express objective of using "the company's capital structure to influence and even drive a change in strategy and culture." Their objective was achieved as the firm "outperformed the S&P 500 by almost 400 percent (or by almost 30 percent per year)."[23]

The second way pertains to a fundamental shift in a firm's offerings. One of the most significant examples of such a redeployment occurred in the mid-1980s when Intel redeployed resources from its historically strong memory chip business into the then nascent microprocessor business. This redeployment optimally positioned

Intel to capitalize on the technology boom that began in the 1990s[24] and continues to this day.[25]

Selling When the Market Price Reflects Underlying Value

Management has a well-known fiduciary duty to maximize a firm's value, but what is less well understood is what is meant by the term "maximize." For instance, it could be interpreted to mean the highest possible price that can conceivably be achieved *or* it could mean a fair price established over a relatively well-defined range based on the firm's fundamentals. The difference between these two interpretations is significant because always striving for the highest possible price is not sustainable and is fraught with risk (consider the well-known historical cases of Lehman Brothers, Enron, and WorldCom). On the other hand, striving for a fundamentally fair price range is much more sustainable, but it requires insight into a firm's value, as well as efficient policies to manage and communicate that value over time.[26] The later approach is practiced, for example, by Berkshire Hathaway, as its chairman and CEO explains:

To the extent possible, we would like each Berkshire shareholder to record a gain or loss in market value during his period of ownership that is proportional to the gain or loss in per-share intrinsic value recorded by the company during that holding period. . . . we would rather see Berkshire's stock price at a *fair* level than a *high* level.[27] Obviously, Charlie [Munger] and I cannot control Berkshire's price. But by our policies and communications, we can encourage informed, rational behavior by owners that, in turn, will tend to produce a stock price that is also rational. Our it's-as-bad-to-be-overvalued-as-to-be-undervalued approach may disappoint some shareholders. We believe, however, that it affords Berkshire the best prospect of attracting long-term investors who seek to profit from the progress of the company rather than from the investment mistakes of their partners (italics added).[28]

Striving for a fair long-term market valuation also facilitates targeted divestment decision-making. Consider the case of the late Henry Singleton's divestments of Teledyne's Argonaut and Unitrin subsidiaries: the decisions behind these divestments were made based on fundamental, financially strategic considerations and thus were extremely well received by the investment community. This example is potentially significant today. For example, 2011's "surge in spin-offs and the rise in the conglomerate discount certainly suggest that new diversifications are likely to be far outweighed by corporate break-ups."[29]

Holding Cash Until Attractive Investments Are Available

Cash is generally ignored strategically. For example, "excess cash"—or cash and marketable securities greater than the short-term needs of a business—is frequently not included in discounted cash flow (DCF) valuations,[30] and it tends to be spent quickly on acquisitions or stock buybacks even at high price levels.[31] In contrast, professional value investors "are willing to hold cash reserves when no bargains are available. . . . The liquidity of cash affords flexibility, for it can quickly be channeled into other investment outlets with minimal transaction costs."[32] For example, Klarman's hedge fund is one of the top performing funds over time even though its cash holdings have averaged 30 percent.[33] In addition, the late Larry Tisch of Loews was described as "having [an] acute radar for a rare investment opportunity, *a ready load of cash*, and the unshakable self-confidence to move swiftly" (italics added).[34] And consider the *2010 Berkshire Hathaway Annual Report*, which states that the firm has "pledged that we will hold at least

$10 billion of cash, excluding that held at our regulated utility and railroad businesses. Because of that commitment, we customarily keep at least $20 billion on hand so that we can both withstand unprecedented insurance losses (our largest to date having been about $3 billion from [Hurricane] Katrina, the insurance industry's most expensive catastrophe) and quickly seize acquisition or investment opportunities, even during times of financial turmoil."[35]

Recommendations and Conclusion

A number of practical things can be done to enable a value investing–based approach to corporate strategy. First, corporate strategists should strive to preserve their capital by actively and economically managing the risk of loss.[36] Indeed, one benefit of margin of safety–based initiatives is that they "carry less risk of loss."[37] As James Grant insightfully explains, "there is safety in cheapness."[38]

Next, most corporate (and investment) managers are assessed on a *relative basis*, which "involves measuring investment results, not against an absolute standard, but against broad stock market indices, such as the Dow Jones Industrial Average or Standard & Poor's 500 Index, or against other investors' results." However, those who assess performance this way "may lose sight of whether their investments are attractive or even sensible in an absolute sense."[39] In contrast, professional value investors focus on *absolute performance* because, simply put, "absolute returns are the only ones that really matter; you cannot, after all, spend relative performance."[40]

Third, "good absolute performance" is achieved by managing over the long term; in other words, it is not focused on the short term.

Fourth, professional value investors assess both risk and reward via *bottom-up analysis*,[41] which involves a careful review of all relevant information in a manner that blends "skepticism and judgment,"[42] which obviously takes time and effort to apply. Top-down analysis, on the other hand, is often much faster and easier to apply (especially when quantitative models are used). The difference between these two approaches is significant, and in many ways it is at the core of why many professional value investors are solvent and buying during times of distress when many other investors are under distress and selling.

Bottom-up analysis is not a panacea—everyone is prone to error. Value investors control for the risk of error by approaching their analyses conservatively, as Klarman explains:

> Since all projections are subject to error, optimistic ones tend to place investors on a precarious limb. Virtually everything must go right, or losses may be sustained. Conservative forecasts can be more easily met or even exceeded. Investors are well advised to make only conservative projections and then invest only at a substantial discount from the valuation derived therefrom [or at a margin of safety].[43]

Finally, corporate managers must ensure that they do not "enhance [strategic uncertainty] by taking unpredictable or ill-considered actions."[44] This means, in part, that when times are bad, and/or when investment opportunities are scarce, cash holdings are accumulated, which is the subject we'll turn to next.

3

Cash and Competitive Advantage

"In the working capital is found the measure of the company's ability to carry on its normal business comfortably and without financial stringency, to expand its operations without the need of new financing, and to meet emergencies and losses without disaster."
—BENJAMIN GRAHAM AND SPENCER MEREDITH[1]

"The secret of success isn't the quality of technology, but the quality of management. It almost goes without saying that the quantity of cash is likewise important."
—JAMES GRANT[2]

ADHERENTS OF WHAT has come to be called "shareholder value maximization theory" often push for the distribution of "excess cash," or cash that is not immediately needed in current operations. The rationale for this position, according to the 2014 Nobel Prize–winning economist Jean Tirole, is that "by taking cash out of [a] firm, it prevents managers from 'consuming' it. That is, it reduces their ability to turn their 'free cash flow' into lavish perks or futile negative net present value investments."[3] Notwithstanding the pejorative nature of this statement, when corporate managers do not have plans for their cash holdings, there is, of course, an argument to be made that an ownership payout is a sensible course of action. For managers with such plans, however, a substantial cash reserve can provide a critical strategic advantage, especially during periods of distress such as a financial crisis.

Cash- and capital-based strategies are period specific. For example, in the 1930s, Benjamin Graham observed, "In the working capital is found the measure of the company's ability to carry on its normal business comfortably and without financial stringency, to expand its operations without the need of new financing, and to meet emergencies and losses without disaster."[4] Given the marketplace of the Great Depression, a focus on cash and the management of liquid assets was clearly understandable.

As the Depression faded from memory, however, focus shifted away from liquid assets to longer-term forms of capital. For example, in 1956, strategist Joe S. Bain published his seminal book, *Barriers to New Competition*, which noted that "absolute capital requirements may be so large that relatively few individuals or groups could secure the needed capital, or that entrants could secure it only at interest rates and other terms which placed them at a net cost disadvantage to established sellers."[5] The strategic nature of capital requirements seems to have been widely recognized up to the beginning of the shareholder value era in 1979.[6] However, that would soon change.

The "Problem" of "Excess Cash"

One consequence of the increasingly easy money environment since the early 1980s is that "capital," broadly defined, is no longer scarce and therefore "capital requirements" no longer tend to be viewed as either a competitive advantage or disadvantage. The higher-order consequences of this development have been significant. For example, consider that so-called "excess cash" is frequently excluded from many M&A valuations:

This excess cash generally represents temporary imbalances in the company's cash flow. For example, the company may build up cash while deciding how to invest or distribute it. These excess cash or marketable securities balances are not generally directly related to the company's operations, so we treat them as non-operating or as financing (negative debt).[7]

The phrase pertaining to "excess cash" not being related to a company's operations can be particularly troubling from a strategic perspective because:

- Running out of cash is a common cause of corporate failures across time,[8] and
- Cash holdings that today appear to be "in excess" may tomorrow be barely adequate to sustain operations, especially if tomorrow brings with it significant levels of distress.

A noted example is the 1998 failure of the infamous hedge fund Long-Term Capital Management (LTCM). Nine months prior to its historic failure, the celebrated managers of the fund, which included two Nobel Prize–winning economists and a former vice-chairman of the Board of Governors of the Federal Reserve System, returned $2.7 billion of capital to their investors, leaving the fund "with a pared-down capital balance of $4,667,953,483." According to journalist Nicholas Dunbar:

> The effect of shrinking the capital base was to increase balance sheet leverage—the ratio of assets to capital—from 18.3 to 27.7. With its $1.25 trillion off-balance-sheet positions, the fund's true leverage was even higher. No one questioned this leverage as excessive. . . . At LTCM's zenith, they had a vision of zero capital and infinite leverage.[9]

Such a strategy culminated in LTCM's historic failure during the financial crisis of 1998, which in many ways was inevitable because, "When bank [or financial] crises come, people don't want accounts in banks: they want cash."[10] This is important because if financial history has taught us anything, it is that there is *always* a next crisis.[11]

Crises, Leverage, and Equity

Crises are obviously not limited to banking, or even to specific industries. Individual firms often fall under distress and fail as a result.[12] For example, most corporate managers appropriately disagree with the concept of "zero capital and infinite leverage," but some nevertheless over-leverage their balance sheets and by so doing risk both "forced selling," or selling at dramatically discounted prices to quickly raise cash,[13] and even failure when the effects of leverage magnify other forms of distress (such as operational disturbances or temporary drop-offs in sales).[14] For example, in a firm that is not leveraged, a 1 percent decline in assets will generally not have a material impact on its operations because that decline equates to only a 1 percent decline in equity. However, in a firm that is excessively leveraged (say, 44 to 1, as Lehman Brothers was prior to its historic failure), a 1 percent decline in assets results in a near 50 percent equity decline.[15] Such a setback would obviously generate significant levels of distress and confusion, which is a reason why, after the 2007–2008 financial crisis, so many people referred to the crisis as a "1-in-100-year event." Such statements were, and are, erroneous as there has been at least one discontinuous financial event every ten years or so, some of which have been even more severe than the 2007–2008 event.[16]

A Timeless Irony

Distress and the resulting need for cash often go hand in hand because at the moment of a crisis—either operational, financial, and/or macroeconomic—firms will often confront "a timeless irony: when you need money most, the most likely sources of it are likely to be hurting as well."[17] The most likely sources of funding are, of course, the capital markets, financial institutions, and trade creditors. When these sources of funding dry up, asset pricing in general, and securities pricing in particular, tend to dramatically decline, providing a strategic opportunity for those with ready cash available. For example, Warren Buffett has built a lucrative career doing exactly this. While his distressed investments in Goldman Sachs and GE during the financial crisis of 2007–2008 are well known,[18] perhaps less well known is that many years prior to that crisis, in 1995, a biographer of his observed, "The trick in such [distressed] markets was to have the cash to exploit the moment—as Buffett put it, 'to have your check clear.'"[19]

Cash and Competitive Advantage

Holding ample cash or what may appear to some—or perhaps even most—to be "excess cash" can be a source of competitive advantage in two different but intimately related ways. First, holding ample cash prior to periods of operational, financial, and/or macroeconomic distress mitigates the risk of becoming a forced seller, and second, it enables a corporate manager to take strategic advantage of others' forced selling. Significantly, there is both contemporary and historical precedent for this type of strategic approach, in addition to the obvious example of Warren Buffett.

Consider the late Larry Tisch, who was the cofounder, chairman, and CEO of Loews Corporation. His biography, which is titled *The King of Cash*, includes this description of his management style:

"Larry Tisch is hard-nosed, a good thinker, and asset-oriented, which at this phase is a lot more than these guys who are interested only in earnings per share." This description, by Smith

45

Barney President Bill Grant in 1971, summarized approvingly Tisch's value-oriented investment style. . . . What Grant envied at least as much about Tisch was liquidity: "He's got one of the greatest reserves of cash in American business today."[20]

This strategy has been maintained at Loews since Jim Tisch took over as CEO. He subsequently noted, "We always wanted to have large amounts of cash on the balance sheet. With cash you can take advantage of opportunities. . . . It's part of the corporate DNA to have cash."[21]

From a historical perspective, consider the case of National City Bank, precursor to today's Citigroup, which emerged from both the Panic of 1893 *and* the Panic of 1907 in a stronger financial position than its competition.[22] As James Stillman, the bank's president at the time, explained to a colleague in early 1907, which was prior to the infamous panic of that year:

> I have felt for some time that the next panic and low interest rates following [it] would straighten out a good many things that have of late years crept into banking. What impresses me as most important is to go into next Autumn (usually a time of financial stringency) ridiculously strong and liquid, and now is the time to begin and shape for it. . . . If by able and judicious management we have money to help our dealers when trust companies have suspended, we will have all the business we want for many years.[23]

And so Stillman and the bank's management did, for as Citigroup's official historians observed, "The bank's performance during the panic capped a remarkable overall achievement. Since 1891, Stillman had built National City from a small treasury unit . . . into the country's foremost commercial bank."[24] One wonders what he would have thought of his firm's management a century later.

Following the 2007–2008 financial crisis, the mathematical models and related technologies upon which many modern financial and risk management functions were built came under intensive popular attack.[25] While some of the criticism is understandable, more focus should have been directed to the strategies underlying how models and their technologies were used, and how those strategies differed from those employed by the firms, including some hedge funds, that actually prospered during the crisis. James Grant performed such an analysis in 2002 after the "new economy" boom went bust, and his insights are seemingly just as applicable today: "The secret of success isn't the quality of technology, but the quality of management. It almost goes without saying that the quantity of cash is likewise important."[26]

Financial Risk and Strategic Uses of Cash

The dramatic rise of financial risk in recent years follows the popularity of "financial innovation," which in many cases pertains to creating financial products that structure funding in ways that mitigate the effects of regulation and/or taxes. There is, of course, nothing nefarious about this as loopholes are included in regulations and tax rules for a reason; however, and as in many kinds of human interactions, there can be unintended consequences with such products.

One consequence is the macroeconomic distress caused by over-leveraged firms exposed to financially innovative products, of which LTCM in 1998 and numerous financial services firms in 2007–2008 are prime examples. A higher order consequence of such exposures is the spillover of financial distress into the real economy. Journalist Roddy Boyd provides an example:

> Given that almost a dozen insurance subs were compromised, millions of policyholders were in danger of literally being at

risk with no economic backing to support their claims. Internationally, there would be an immediate slowdown to shipping and aviation, as AIG was a key player in insuring both market segments. . . . Financially, it would have been true chaos. What cash or liquid assets there was at AIG would have been sent, eventually, to the insurance subsidiaries to meet those obligations. Left remaining would have been a $1.2 trillion balance sheet that would have dwarfed the collapse from the looming Lehman bankruptcy.[27]

During periods of distress, cash shortages generally result from the interaction of three factors: a dramatic decline in cash flow from operations, an inadequate stock of cash on the balance sheet, and insufficient/ineffectual hedges. Firms suffering cash shortages are vulnerable to competitors who are better positioned—or "cash rich"—during a crisis. This key lesson of financial history can be strategically employed by a wide variety of corporate managers.

Conclusion

The following four practical steps enable a competitive cash advantage:

1. Balance sheet implications. Corporate managers should consider the interactive dynamics of the left and right sides of their balance sheets. For example, firms that "lend long and borrow short" would obviously benefit from a strong cash position over time. Another example is the use of leverage: operational leverage can be very positive and help firms become more efficient. Financial leverage, on the other hand, can be a "double-edged sword" as it magnifies profitability during good times, but it intensifies losses during periods of distress, as the examples above illustrate.

2. Assess competitors' balance sheets. Corporate managers should then assess the interactive dynamics of their key competitors' balance sheets, paying particular attention to competitors that seem to be overextending themselves. A master of this kind of analysis is John C. Malone, who has "relished the role of bargain hunter amid the spoils of bad deals made by his competitors."[28]

3. Scenario analysis. A form of scenario planning can then be used to identify a set of existential conditions that would affect both the left-hand and right-hand sides of your balance sheet. For example, strategists can create scenarios that depict the simultaneous write-down of significant accounts receivable and inventories along with some form of credit impairment that disrupts funding requirements. Once such scenarios are identified, corporate managers can then scan the environment to determine if such "unwanted futures" are actually developing.[29]

4. Competitor scenarios. The same kind of scenario analysis on key competitors can then be conducted.[30] If a firm observes that one or more of its competitors' are likely to find themselves in an "unwanted future"—for example, the stress that Bear Sterns was under before it failed—it is time to further strengthen its own cash position based on two objectives: first, not to become a forced seller in the advent of stressful macroeconomic and/or operational distress, and second, to position itself to take strategic advantage of any competitor's forced selling, such as JP Morgan's distressed acquisition of Bear Sterns during the 2007–2008 financial crisis.

This form of strategic scenario analysis should not be confused with the "realistic disaster scenario" (RDS) practice. An RDS is a modeled loss that, in theory, is meant to portray some statistical "worst case" scenario at a given level of confidence. In practice, such scenarios tend not to be very actionable in that they do not help identify potential strategic or bargain-priced opportunities that can result from distress.

In closing, cash is a strategic resource and, like all strategic resources, it can be used wisely or unwisely.[31] When it is used unwisely, a firm's cash holdings can be used against it by helping to fund a takeover.[32] Therefore, holding ample cash is only a first step; determining how it will be strategically deployed, and how the strategy will be communicated to capital providers, are critical next steps. Firms such as Loews and Berkshire Hathaway provide ready examples for further study.

4

Corporate Management and "Security Analysis"

"It is at least as important to the stockholders that they be able to obtain a fair price for their shares as it is that the dividends, earnings, and assets be conserved and increased. It follows that the responsibility of managements to act in the interest of their shareholders includes the obligation to prevent—insofar as they are able—the establishment of either absurdly high or unduly low prices for their securities."
—BENJAMIN GRAHAM AND DAVID DODD[1]

"While some might mistakenly consider value investing a mechanical tool for identifying bargains, it is actually a comprehensive investment philosophy that emphasizes the need to perform in-depth fundamental analysis, pursue long-term investment results, limit risk, and resist crowd psychology."
—SETH A. KLARMAN[2]

DESPITE THE LONG–TERM success of professional value investors such as Warren Buffett, the late Marty Whitman, Mario Gabelli, Lee Cooperman, Seth Klarman, and Mitch Julis, value investing has thus far had nowhere near the same level of influence on corporate management. This is curious, especially when you consider Warren Buffett's comments that he is a better investor because he is a businessman and a better businessman because he is an investor.[3]

When the sixth edition of *Security Analysis* was published in 2009, I had the opportunity to review it from a corporate management perspective. Here are the first and most obvious areas where value investing can influence corporate management:

- Mergers and acquisitions (M&A)[4]
- Firms with substantial fixed income holdings, such as financial institutions, can apply value investing to improve the performance of their portfolios beyond traditional institutional asset allocation strategies.[5] This is not as easy as it may seem. As noted earlier in this book, institutional asset allocators and value investors see the world very differently, and in some firms, this difference cannot be reconciled. But therein lies an opportunity for firms that can reconcile it.
- Formulating value–based dividend and share repurchase policies
- Taking a value–based approach to investor relations[6]
- Appreciating the influence of history on the economy and business cycle[7]

However, the lessons of the latest edition of *Security Analysis* extend far beyond the above applications. Consider the following:

- Corporate managers can leverage value investing's bottom-up analytical approach to more insightfully question the assumptions and conventional wisdom of a wide range of business activities. For example, there is a reason why professional value investors generally were not caught up in the subprime/structured finance mess that affected so many other investors and firms in 2007–2008. When performed properly, the approach is designed to evaluate each investment based on "the facts," which may be informed by external credit ratings, analyst rankings, etc., but are *not* dependent on them.
- Maintaining a conservative capital structure and, at times, ample cash holdings, as discussed in **Chapter 3**.

- Integrating capital expenditures with focused strategic management initiatives to leverage brand strength and other competitive advantages of a *franchise*, which is value investing nomenclature of a firm with a sustainable competitive advantage.[8]

Security Analysis also provides other practical considerations that could be leveraged from a corporate governance perspective:

- Efficiently managing a firm's value drivers while economically mitigating its risk drivers, and
- Better understanding the financial implications of options,[9] compensation policies, and other incentives that could impact a firm's value.

The sixth edition of *Security Analysis* is based on the classic 1940 (second) edition of the work, which is highly detailed. Because the examples are obviously dated, each section in the new edition opens with an essay written by a successful modern value investor. For example, Seth Klarman—the book's lead editor—opens with a detailed introduction on the applicability of *Security Analysis* to modern investing.[10] James Grant follows with the historical backdrop of Benjamin Graham and *Security Analysis*.[11] Additional sections were written by Howard Marks on fixed income/credit analysis,[12] Professor Bruce Greenwald on balance sheet analysis, which in many ways is the foundation of value investing, and which could prove to be very important to modern corporate managers,[13] Roger Lowenstein (who is also the author of a biography of Warren Buffett),[14] and others.

Shortly after I drafted the article that preceded this chapter, I posed some questions on the topic of value investing and corporate management to Seth Klarman:

Question: In your long and successful career as a value investor, what do you think is the most important lesson corporate managers can learn from *Security Analysis* today?

Answer: Simply put, Graham and Dodd's *margin of safety* concept.[15] If executives managed their businesses by this concept they would not fall prey to suboptimal M&A deals, or debacles such as those generated from junk bonds, structured finance, etc.

There seem to be two major reasons why the margin of safety has not been more widely adopted in corporate management. The first is psychological; meaning, the margin of safety seems to either immediately resonate with someone or they tend to view the world differently. As Warren Buffett observed, "It is extraordinary to me that the idea of buying dollar bills for 40 cents takes immediately with people or it doesn't take at all. It's like an inoculation. If it doesn't grab a person right away, I find that you can talk to him for years and show him records, and it doesn't make any difference. They just don't seem able to grasp the concept, simple as it is."[16] Another way of saying this is that most people seem psychologically oriented to speculative–based approaches irrespective of the risks those approaches may generate over time.

The second reason pertains to issues of agency. For example, if incentives are in place to reward executives—by way of larger salaries and bonuses, etc.—for managing a bigger firm, then many executives will respond to those incentives irrespective of whether their activities contain a margin of safety or not. This, for instance, provides a rationale for some corporate M&A activity, which is conducted in the face of widespread knowledge that many M&A deals fail, and that many of those failures are caused by simply paying too much.[17]

Question: Can you comment on Graham and Dodd's concepts of investment and speculation, and how those concepts potentially apply to the financial crises of 2007–2008 in a corporate management context?

Answer: Along with the margin of safety, understanding the differences between investment and speculation is absolutely core to the Graham and Dodd approach. For example, because of the margin of safety concept, Graham and Dodd–based valuations are inherently conservative thereby enabling value investors to better manage the risk of loss over time. Furthermore, Graham and Dodd valuations are formulated from the bottom-up utilizing both quantitative and qualitative information, and therefore are very fact–based. Because of this, value investors avoid the risks inherent in high momentum issues (which do not provide a margin of safety, and as such are risky and therefore avoided). Roger Lowenstein's example of Washington Mutual (WaMu) in our book is a contemporary, and dramatic, example of this.[18]

It is very easy to speculate and chase yield when: (1) markets are running, (2) research reports present seemingly "risk-free" investment alternatives, and (3) investment standards are noticeably slipping in the face of seemingly consistent impressive returns. It is far more difficult to be patient at such times even when you know that the risk of speculation far outweighs the returns offered; however, that is exactly what value investors as a group do. Warren Buffett, for example, showed the utility of this approach recently (in mid-to-late 2008),[19] as have many other value investors.

Question: As *Security Analysis* was written during a time of substantial financial volatility, which we seem to be experiencing again (as of 2009), do you hope to see a broader application of the Graham and Dodd approach in the field of corporate management as opposed to just investment management?

Answer: Managers have many performance levers to choose from; Graham and Dodd can help them select the right levers at the right time. For example, managers of publicly held firms must decide whether to expand their business offerings or whether to buy back shares on the market. If a particular firm's stock price is depressed, from a value investing perspective a share buy-back is an optimal use of capital. Conversely, if a firm's stock is priced high on the market it could be used on a targeted basis to economically expand the business offering. This is exactly the type of approach that Henry Singleton, the late CEO of Teledyne, utilized so successfully. Dr. Singleton was so successful, in fact, that Warren Buffett considered him to have "the best operating and capital deployment record in American business."[20]

In order to successfully carry out activities like those described above, managers must have a disciplined method for valuing their businesses, which *Security Analysis* will provide them. Significantly, Graham and Dodd valuations are conservatively prepared in the context of a longer-term time horizon, which is useful from a management perspective. For example, firms that used popular academic models like the Capital Asset Pricing Model (CAPM) in 2008 saw their cost of capital estimates skyrocket, and therefore if the executives of those firms were managing to such models their operations likely suffered. Conversely, value investors do not use models like the CAPM because they confuse volatility, which can be period sensitive, with the risk of loss.[21] By focusing on the risks and returns of specific businesses, conservatively assessed, value investors are able to act decisively when models like the CAPM break down, which is typically when margin of safety–rich investment opportunities are offered. Businessmen like Warren Buffett and the late Henry Singleton clearly understand (understood) this, and the results they achieved clearly reflect that understanding.

In closing, when we began this project two years ago (circa 2007) it was our intention to produce a long-lasting edition that would contribute to the literature from both an investment and a business perspective. As you noted above, Benjamin Graham and David Dodd published the first edition of this classic book in 1934. Ironically, the economy of 2008–2009 is starting to somewhat resemble the economy of 1934, which only supports the position that value investing is as relevant today as it was then, for both investors and corporate managers alike.

5

Value Creating Corporate Management: Henry E. Singleton

"According to [Warren] Buffett, if one took the top 100 business school graduates and made a composite of their triumphs, their record would not be as good as that of [Henry] Singleton. . . . The failure of business schools to study men like Singleton is a crime, he says."
—JOHN TRAIN[1]

"Something went haywire with American Capitalism in the 1990s, and we think we know what it is. There weren't enough Henry E. Singletons to go around. In truth, there was only one Singleton, and he died before 1999. . . . He habitually bought low and sold high. The study of such a protean thinker and doer is always worthwhile. Especially is it valuable today, a time when the phrase 'great capitalist' has almost become an oxymoron."
—JAMES GRANT[2]

IN THE ABOVE INTERVIEW, Seth Klarman referenced the late Henry Singleton. When I asked him for more information, he referred me to Lee Cooperman, the founder, CEO, and chairman of Omega Advisors, Inc. Before I reached out to Mr. Cooperman, I accumulated as much information as I could find on Singleton, which was somewhat difficult as he was a very private man who did not write a memoir. However, his number two at Teledyne— George Roberts—did write one. In 2007, Roberts self-published *Distant Force: A Memoir of the Teledyne Corporation and the Man Who Created It*. While this book was helpful for background purposes, Cooperman provided greater detail since he both knew

Singleton personally and invested in Teledyne for twenty-five years. By drawing on these sources, I hope to show how Singleton's actions are a classic case of value investing–based corporate management in action.

Background and Approach

Henry Singleton's academic training was in engineering and included a doctorate from the Massachusetts Institute of Technology. With this background he logically chose to focus his business activities on emerging, innovative technologies;[3] in other words, he made technology Teledyne's core competency.

Singleton built his firm on a very strong balance sheet,[4] which is important because balance sheet analysis and management have generally become something of a lost art. The lack of balance sheet understanding has unfortunately resulted in significant losses over the years. For example, in *The Big Short*, journalist Michael Lewis profiled investors who were short financial services firms prior to the 2007–2008 financial crisis; in essence, these investors wagered that the value of certain financial services' securities would decline and they profited handsomely when that wager proved correct. What caused these investors to take such a highly contrarian view at the time? One of the profiled investors indicated that he would, "go to meetings with Wall Street CEOs and ask them the most basic questions about their balance sheets. 'They didn't know,' he said. 'They didn't know their own balance sheets.' "[5] Contrast this statement with the one Lee Cooperman made about Teledyne in 1982 (when he was a Goldman Sachs analyst):

At a time when American industry is saddled with the most illiquid financial position and highest debt load in the post–World War II period, Teledyne is in its most liquid financial position ever. . . . The company currently has cash and cash equivalents of nearly $1 billion, no bank debt, and less than $5 million *per year* of maturing long-term debt in the ten-year period, 1984–1993. In addition, at recent levels of profitability, the company (*excluding* noncash equity accounting earnings) generates approximately $400 million per year of cash flow.[6]

Off his clean balance sheet, Singleton employed innovative financial strategies to realize value, which is arguably the area that he is best known for today. For example, he successfully diversified into financial services, and he employed stock buybacks and spin-offs strategically.

Corporate management requires both analytical decision-making and sound professional judgment. There are generally two ways to develop judgment: experience and historical study. As an industrialist, Singleton "was a student and an observer of the history of manufacturing. He studied the progress and growth of corporations from the days of Henry Ford to General Motors and how successful corporations grew by acquisitions. He studied the behavior of Jimmy Ling and others who were beginning to grow in this manner.[7] He studied the emerging conglomerates Litton, TRW, LTVs, City Investing, Gulf and Western, and General Electric."[8]

Singleton also used history strategically; for example, after reading Alfred Sloan's classic memoir, *My Years at General Motors*, he realized that "for a corporation to grow and to have a strong financial base, it needed to have, as part of itself, an interest in substantial financially oriented institutions."[9] Therefore, Teledyne augmented its technological core competency with insurance businesses, which Singleton managed remarkably well.

He also executed strategy very flexibly by not managing to a formal business plan. "Once criticized for not having a business plan, Henry replied that he knew that a lot of people running companies had very definite plans they followed assiduously. 'But we're subject to a great number of outside influences on our businesses, and most of them can't be predicted. So my plan is to stay flexible.'"[10]

Operationally, Singleton was hands-on. A Teledyne employee remembered once preparing a newly developed navigation system for a demonstration "when suddenly he realized that Henry Singleton was on his hands and knees alongside him helping to get the system up and running. 'I was very surprised. Here was a brilliant man with a doctorate in electrical engineering who undoubtedly knew more about electronics than I would ever learn, helping me put this system together. . . . From a leadership standpoint, that was really a lesson for me.'"[11]

Singleton looked for similar traits in the managers he hired; for example, after George Roberts joined Teledyne, Singleton introduced him to one of his managers whom he described like this:

> What's unique about him is that I'll ask him a question about one of those companies that I've asked him to supervise, and he always knows the exact numerical answer. If I ask him what they did in sales last month, he knows right away without calling someone to find out.
>
> So . . . that's the kind of fellow that you pick who runs a company and does it well, but is also able to quickly understand and supervise, and have the facts about other companies under his wing. That's the kind of a group leader we need.[12]

So important was managerial skill to Singleton that he formulated a "management inventory" to ensure that Teledyne was "collecting and promoting the right people." He also incorporated management expertise into his M&A criteria many years before doing so became popular.[13]

Financial Strategy

As noted above, Singleton is perhaps best known for his expertise in the area of financial strategy. The outlook underlying his success in this area was distinctly long-term; for example, in 1987, which was toward the end of his career, he was asked a series of questions for a *Financial World* magazine article. The questions were intended to gain insight into how management was going to boost Teledyne's stock price, presumably in the near future. He replied characteristically that he was "not particularly persuaded by quick temporary gains. We'd rather get something permanent. And it takes time." Questioned further on this topic he replied more firmly, "You're thinking in the short-term, I'm in the long-term. So I wouldn't do anything . . . for a temporary rise in the price of a stock."[14] These replies are very relevant today, especially for corporate managers who manage to the short term, which is a tendency that is so prevalent that even some mainstream academic economists are seeking to change it.[15]

A long-term outlook facilitates allocative efficiency, which exemplified Singleton's managerial approach. For example, Warren Buffett felt that Singleton had "the best operating and capital deployment record in American business."[16] To understand why, consider that he grew Teledyne through acquisitions, but he only did so when M&A pricing was favorable. His acquisition criteria are still relevant today:

1) Is the company (i.e., target) profitable?
2) Do they have a good balance sheet?
3) Is their profit and loss statement accurate?
4) Do they have clean inventory?
5) Is their backlog realistic and well documented?
6) Is their management on top of their operations?
7) Have they made long-range plans to maximize their profit in a sellout?
8) Does the business have growth potential?
9) Is there opportunity for growth in profit?
10) Can cash be taken from the company for use elsewhere?
11) How is depreciation counted and is it a significant percentage of profits?

12) What is the condition of their physical plant?
13) And finally, and probably most important: Would this company be a good fit within the Teledyne organization and its goals?[17]

Despite his many M&A successes, when private market valuations increased and acquisitions were no longer economical, Singleton stopped acquiring. Even though such a decision is highly "rational," it was highly contrarian at the time—as, indeed, it would be at the present time (mid-2018) given how high prices are at the time of this writing[18]—as many other corporate managers at the time, including the popular Harold Geneen of ITT, were still acquiring. Singleton explained his rationale to *Forbes* magazine in 1978: "I won't pay 15 times earnings. That would mean I'd only be making a return of 6 or 7 percent.[19] I can do that in T-bills. We don't have to make any major acquisitions. We have other things we are busy doing." Those "other things" included buying securities of select firms when stock pricing was favorable, in contrast to acquisition pricing, and he used the reserves of Teledyne's insurance companies to help fund the purchases.[20] This strategy worked so well that, at the time, Teledyne was the largest stockholder of nine *Fortune 500* companies and it had effective control of six of them.[21]

Singleton was also one of the first corporate managers to use stock buybacks strategically; that is, he bought back Teledyne stock when its price was *low*. Contrast this with more current practices: "In 2006 and 2007 alone, U.S. nonfinancial corporations borrowed roughly $1.3 trillion—much of it for the express purpose of funding share repurchases at a time when stock prices were nearing record highs."[22] To understand the differences in each approach, first consider Teledyne's buyback history from its beginning on September 14, 1972, to its conclusion on May 9, 1984, which resulted in a cumulative 85.4 percent buyback of outstanding shares.[23]

The buyback activity can be separated into two phases, with each phase employing a different financial strategy. Phase 1, from

September 14, 1972, to February 6, 1976, resulted in a 67.4 percent buyback of outstanding shares,[24] after Singleton bought back Teledyne stock that was undervalued due to bear market conditions. He recounted the success of this strategy in 1979:

> In October 1972 we tendered for 1 million shares and 8.9 million came in. We took them all at $20 [per share] and figured that was a fluke, and that we couldn't do it again. But instead of going up, our stock went down. So we kept tendering, first at $14 and then doing bond-for-stock swaps. Every time one tender was over the stock would go down and we'd tender again, and we'd get a new deluge. Then two more tenders at $18 and $40.[25]

Phase 2, from May 2, 1980, to May 9, 1984, resulted in the buyback of the final 18 percent of outstanding shares (for a total of 85.4 percent),[26] after the buybacks were pursued due to Teledyne stock being undervalued on a more relative basis. To explain, consider the 1980 tender, which was a bond-for-stock swap. That tender was made when interest rates were at their highest point of the year, as shown in **Figure 5.1**, and thus undervalued equity was economically swapped for favorably priced debt.[27] How did he accomplish this? While the details seem lost to history, consider this revealing quote by a former Teledyne executive: "[Dr. Singleton] spends his time thinking and reading books, and is not interested in chit-chat. He is interested in grappling with major intellectual, technical and financial matters—like *A History of Interest Rates*, which he was reading that day."[28]

Now consider Teledyne's 1984 stock buyback, which is profiled in **Table 5.1**. Despite having $1.74 billion *less equity* after the buyback (cell c2 in the exhibit), Teledyne's market capitalization *increased* by $318.3 million (cell e4 in the exhibit) in just ninety days. Furthermore, the buyback was funded with cash, not debt.

Throughout all of Teledyne's tenders, Singleton never sold a single share of his stock; rather, he watched his ownership percentage

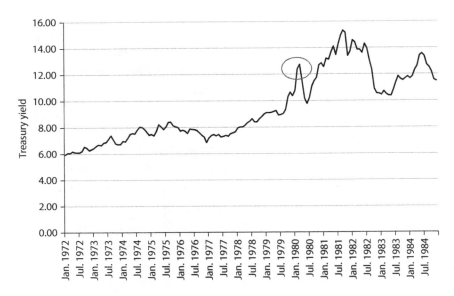

FIGURE 5.1 10-year Treasury Yield (%): 1972 to 1984. *Note*: The above circle denotes Treasury yields at the time of Teledyne's May 1980 tender per Leon G. Cooperman, *A Case Study in Financial Brilliance: Teledyne, Inc., Dr. Henry E. Singleton* (November 28, 2007a): 8. *Data source*: U.S. Federal Reserve System.

Table 5.1
Teledyne May 1984 Stock Buyback

	Price per Share	Shares Outstanding	Market Cap or Buyback Cost	New Shares Outstanding	Value Created
	(a)	(b)	(c) = (a)*(b)	(d) = (b1) − (b2)	(e) = (c4) − (c1
(1) **May 9, 1984 close**	$155.75	20,300,000	$3,161,725,000		
(2) **Buyback**	$200.00	8,700,000	$1,740,000,000		
(3) **New Shares Outstanding**				11,600,000	
(4) **90 Days Later**	$300.00	11,600,000	$3,480,000,000		$318,275,000

Data source: Leon G. Cooperman, *A Case Study in Financial Brilliance: Teledyne, Inc., Dr. Henry E. Singleton*, November 2? 2007, 10. Calculations are mine and have been rounded.

steadily increase, as did all long-term Teledyne shareholders. (See **Appendix 5.1** for information on "Evaluating a Stock Buyback," which is based on value investor Lee Cooperman's research.)

In addition to stock buybacks, Singleton spun off business units strategically—that is, when the value of doing so was greater than the value of continuing to manage them within Teledyne. For example, he spun off Teledyne's Argonaut Insurance Group in 1986 for $234 million (a 169 percent gain based on the 1969 acquisition price).[29] *Barron's* made this observation after Singleton spun off the rest of Teledyne's insurance companies in 1990:

> Spin-offs, of course, are now familiar on Wall Street, but what makes this one a little different is that it represents another in a long series of moves by Singleton to enrich his shareholders. While other companies spend a lot of time talking about "maximizing shareholder value," Singleton's company has a history of doing just that.[30]

Toward the end of his career, Singleton split Teledyne into three separate groups "to provide shareholders a choice of concentration of their holdings in areas of their greatest interest."[31] Incentives also motivated this restructuring. For example, Singleton did not believe it was rational to base a technologist's compensation in part on how an insurance company performed.[32] As a result, splitting Teledyne into specific groups facilitated more focused management structures and incentive compensation programs.

Conclusion

In his study of Teledyne, Cooperman outlined the five core phases of its strategy as follows:

Phase 1: 1961–1969: Growth through acquisition
Phase 2: 1970–1981: Intensively manage the business

Phase 3: 1972–1984: Repurchase undervalued equity
Phase 4: 1976–1982: Stocks preferable to bonds because of the tax advantage for investors
Phase 5: 1986–1992: Simplify the corporate structure and focus on management[33]

In each phase, Singleton did not preach to the media or to Wall Street, both of which he frequently ignored.[34] As such, he was the quintessential "quiet leader." According to Professor Joseph Badaracco, "quiet leadership is a long, hard race, run on obscure pathways, not a thrilling sprint before a cheering crowd."[35] The customers, shareholders, and employees of Teledyne were extremely fortunate they had such a leader, as the historical performance of Teledyne illustrates in **Table 5.2**.

By way of comparison, the late Marty Whitman included Teledyne in a comparative study he prepared for another corporate manager, which is reproduced in **Table 5.3**.

Despite such stellar results, Teledyne was not profiled in Jim Collins's once popular business book *Good to Great* because Singleton "had not prepared a successor when he retired, and thus the return to shareholders declined abruptly at that point."[36] Instead, Collins profiled, among other firms, Fannie Mae, which failed in the 2007–2008 financial crisis.[37] Singleton's general omission from strategy, leadership, and finance–based research is illogical.[38] Consider not only the results he produced, but also the following points:

- In a 1979 article, *Forbes* observed, "When the business history of this era is written, Dr. Henry E. Singleton will probably be one of its towering figures, the equal of accomplishments, if not in fame, of great corporate entrepreneurs like Alfred P. Sloan, Jr., Gerard Swope, David Sarnoff, Royal Little."[39]
- In 2008, James Grant observed, "Singleton did well what so many corporate managements today do badly: When

Table 5.2
Teledyne's Historical Performance

Year	Sales	Net Income	Net Income per Share	Assets	Shareholders' Equity
1986	$3,241.4	$238.3	$20.35	$2,744.2	$1,636.6
1985	3,256.2	546.4	46.66	2,775.4	1,577.4
1984	3,494.3	574.3	37.69	2,790.7	1,159.3
1983	2,979.0	304.6	14.87	3,852.2	2,641.2
1982	2,863.8	269.6	13.05	3,290.7	2,111.1
1981	3,237.6	421.9	20.43	2,904.5	1,723.2
1980	2,926.4	352.4	15.62	2,575.9	1,410.2
1979	2,705.6	379.6	15.02	2,050.8	1,288.6
1978	2,441.6	254.4	9.63	1,588.2	890.3
1977	2,209.7	201.3	7.53	1,443.1	702.2
1976	1,937.6	137.6	4.78	1,228.5	516.1
1975	1,715.0	101.7	2.57	1,136.5	489.3
1974	1,700.0	31.5	0.55	1,108.9	477.8
1973	1,455.5	66.0	1.01	1,227.4	532.8
1972	1,216.0	59.3	0.67	1,127.8	484.0
1971	1,101.9	57.4	0.62	1,964.8	606.1
1970	1,216.4	61.9	0.69	952.6	576.3
1969	1,294.8	58.1	0.68	938.1	502.0
1968	806.7	40.3	0.56	602.4	316.5
1967	451.1	21.3	0.38	336.7	152.6
1966	256.8	12.0	0.29	170.4	90.2
1965	86.5	3.4	0.16	66.5	34.8
1964	38.2	1.4	0.10	35.0	13.7
1963	31.9	0.7	0.06	23.9	8.6
1962	10.4	0.2	0.02	10.8	3.5
1961	4.5	0.1	0.01	3.7	2.5

Source: Leon G. Cooperman, *A Case Study in Financial Brilliance: Teledyne, Inc., Dr. Henry E. Singleton*, November 28, 2007, 4. Dollars in millions except per share values.

Table 5.3
Teledyne's Relative Performance

	Earnings per Share			Net Asset Value per Share		
Issuer	*1984*	*1975*	*Change*	*1984*	*1975*	*Change*
GATX	$2.37	$3.47	–32%	$30.35[a]	$32.22[a]	–6%
Crown Cork & Seal	$4.98	$2.43	105%	$40.61[b]	$14.32[b]	184%
Tandy	$2.75	$0.25	1,000%	$10.64[a]	$1.33[a]	700%
Teledyne	**$20.61**	**$2.57**	**702%**	**$123.36[b]**	**$9.57[b]**	**1,189%**

Notes:
[a] Excludes the value of extraordinary distributions of the common stocks of subsidiaries.
[b] 10 years to December 31, 1983.
Source: Martin J. Whitman, *Value Investing: A Balanced Approach* (New York: Wiley, 1999), 257. Change percentages and boldface font were added by me and have been rounded.

Teledyne shares were richly valued, he used them as currency with which to make acquisitions. But when the cycle turned and the shares got cheap, he repurchased and retired them. Tendering for his company's own stock between 1972 and 1984, . . . he reduced the Teledyne share count by 90 percent. Singleton took no options awards and bought his own stock with his own money. He sold none of his personal holdings. A model capitalist indeed!"[40]

- In an interview, Cooperman told me that Singleton was the most successful corporate manager he ever met.[41]
- In addition, Warren Buffett stated in a letter to Cooperman that "Henry [Singleton] is a manager that all investors, CEOs, would be CEOs, and MBA students should study."[42]

Evaluating a Stock Buyback

"The payment of an exceedingly liberal price for expected future improvement—in the form of a very high multiplier of past or current earnings—is hardly a businesslike procedure."
—BENJAMIN GRAHAM, DAVID DODD, AND SIDNEY COTTLE[1]

"Repurchasing stock is rational only if the intrinsic value of the company is higher than the market price."
—ROBERT HAGSTROM[2]

IN ADDITION TO HIS STUDY of Henry Singleton, Lee Cooperman also studied the buyback strategy of Loews Corporation, which employs a similar buyback strategy in that they buy back undervalued shares, *not* fairly valued or overvalued ones.[3] Significantly, the celebrated media executive John Malone engaged in similar behavior. According to a biographer, "Malone decided on a familiar strategy he employed whenever he thought the market had undervalued his company's shares: He bought back Liberty Media shares. If you believe the share price is cheap, Malone liked to say, why not buy back your own shares at a bargain?"[4]

Regardless of the above examples, many corporate managers do not buy back their shares at a bargain. For example, in *Investing Between the Lines*, L. J. Rittenhouse observed "that between 2001 and 2010, on average, 34 percent of all Rittenhouse Rankings survey companies reported on share repurchases. However, only 4 percent reported on buying back *undervalued* shares" (italics original).[5] Such uneconomical buying did not end in 2010.

In the March 7, 2014, edition of *Grant's Interest Rate Observer*, editor James Grant observed,

> According to FactSet, the average price at which the companies of the S&P 500 repurchased stock between the fourth quarter of 2012 and the third quarter of 2013 was 99.8 percent of the average price for the preceding 12 months. In other words, managements bought in shares not because the price was low, or the value commanding. They bought in shares, as we read the managerial mind, because everyone else was buying them in. Share repurchases, their use and especially abuse, is the subject at hand. . . . In the third quarter of 2013, the latest period for which complete data are available, S&P 500 companies repurchased $123.9 billions' worth of stock, down a hair from the second quarter but 32 percent higher than the like period in 2012.[6]

Why do some (many) corporate managers continue to "buy high" when history's most successful investors and corporate managers have demonstrated that the way to profit consistently over the long term is to do the exact opposite?[7] I believe the answer involves elements of herding and fixating on the short term, which interact to generate such behavior.[8] Whatever the actual reason(s), corporate managers, and the boards that oversee them, can follow an alternative path. In the case of share buybacks, Cooperman created the following criteria to inform such decisions:

1) Are we buying back stock at a discount from private market value or merger market value?[9]
2) Do we have a growing business that will be worth more over time? For example, what does our five-year budget produce in the way of a discounted cash flow? Are we buying back stock at a discount (e.g., 15–20 percent) of that value?

3) What does the buyback add to our cash flow and earnings per share?

4) Will the buyback radically change the firm's risk profile? If so, it should not be pursued.[10]

The disciplined, consistent application of criteria like these will help to prevent "the payment of an exceedingly liberal price for expected future improvement—in the form of a very high multiplier of past or current earnings," to cite the quotation from Benjamin Graham, David Dodd, and Sidney Cottle that opened this appendix.

Managing Funding Obligations

"Financial difficulties are almost always heralded by the presence
of bank loans or of other debt due in a short time. In other
words, it is rare for a weak financial position to be created solely
by ordinary trade accounts."
—BENJAMIN GRAHAM AND DAVID DODD[1]

"The late Melchior Palyi defined liquidity as the 'capacity to
fulfill financial obligations.' The world can hardly be said to
be awash with that, any more than it can be said to be awash
with prudence."
—JAMES GRANT[2]

CONSIDERING WHETHER to buy back stock falls within the scope
of the larger category of funding obligations management, which
involves multiple considerations including working capital, interest coverage, terms and conditions (such as maturity management,
covenants, and call provisions), preferred dividends, common dividends, share count, incentive compensation, and retained earnings.
Taken together, these obligations are generated from the capital
structure designed to fund corporate activities, which has *always*
been a significant managerial responsibility. However, as already
noted, many mainstream academic economists continue to believe
that capital structure is "irrelevant."[3] The consequences stemming
from this belief have been significant and, in some cases, tragic.

First, some corporate managers simply do not know their own
balance sheets.[4] Second, even those who do know their balance
sheets may not understand the dynamics that could be generated

from them. A dramatic example of this lack of understanding was the failure of Long-Term Capital Management (LTCM) in 1998. While a great deal has been written about this failure, Robert Merton—one of LTCM's principals and a Nobel Prize–winning economist—was asked in 2012 what he learned as a result of the failure; his response was enlightening. He cogently explained that while LTCM's funding was termed out, it was subject to collateral on a mark-to-market basis that, given the volatility of Russia's default in 1998, resulted in a positive feedback loop that caused the firm to fail, which he claimed he could not have foreseen.[5]

I have discussed the LTCM failure with many corporate managers, and some of them noted, with a wink and a smile, "Well, what would you expect from a bunch of economists?" Perhaps, but we witnessed similar failures during 2007–2008 at firms not led by economists. Furthermore, throughout history even some of the smartest and most innovative business owners have failed for similar reasons. Consider Thomas Edison and George Westinghouse. Their genius is widely acknowledged, yet each man famously lost control of the firm he founded for funding reasons:

- Thomas Edison lost control of Edison General Electric in 1892 after J. P. Morgan restructured the firm's "sizable floating debt."[6] After the restructuring, the firm was rebranded General Electric.
- George Westinghouse lost control of Westinghouse Electric shortly after the famous Panic of 1907 due to "the floating debt [that] had climbed about $14 million, much of it maturing soon [at the time]."[7]

In his classic study of the era of Edison and Westinghouse, business historian Maury Klein observed, "Everywhere it seemed that bankers were coming in and taking over enterprises once ruled by their creators."[8] In sum, capital structure matters. It always has and it always will,[9] and therefore it *must* be carefully managed.[10]

6

Managerial "Rationality"

"The main obstacles to the success of the analyst's work are
threefold: (1) the inadequacy or incorrectness of the data,
(2) the uncertainties of the future, and (3) the irrational behavior
of the market."
—BENJAMIN GRAHAM AND DAVID DODD[1]

"Most of the time common stocks are subject to irrational and
excessive price fluctuations in both directions, as the consequence
of the ingrained tendency of most people to speculate or gamble—
i.e., to give way to hope, fear and greed."
—BENJAMIN GRAHAM (ITALICS ORIGINAL)[2]

THE WORD "RATIONAL" has been used several times in this book
and, indeed, the subject of "rationality" often comes up in investment discussions. It also appears in Warren Buffett's writings; for
example, when I spoke with Lee Cooperman during the research for
the last chapter, he referred to a letter Buffett wrote him regarding
Henry Singleton's managerial behavior. In that letter, he referred to
Singleton as being "100 percent rational,"[3] which seemed to be an
important statement depending on how rational was being defined.

In this chapter, I will profile three general definitions of the
term "rationality" and then demonstrate how one of these definitions can be practically employed in both corporate and investment management. I will show this via historical profiles of two
corporate managers who publicly declared their intention to create shareholder value. Managers often make such declarations,
but not all managers follow through, and for those who do, there

is wide variation in value creation effectiveness, especially over time. Therefore, insight into when such declarations have a higher probability of being realized could help to inform investment and strategic analyses.

Given the profile nature of this chapter, I do not intend to thoroughly survey or examine the intricacies of either the concept of rationality or corporate management in general. Rather, my intention is to introduce the concept of rationality and then to profile its usefulness.

Definition Overview

Economists generally hold that expectations are "rational" when they are expected to generate correct decisions but for the presence of random error. One problem with this definition is that many nonrandom erroneous decisions have been made over time, including erroneous managerial and investment decisions. For a historical example, consider that over one hundred years ago, an early biography of J. P. Morgan made this observation:

> The theory of competition contains the assumption, accepted for over a century, that when the returns from an undertaking fall below the cost of service, competition will come to an end. According to the school books no railroad could afford to carry freight and passengers for less than cost, and would not attempt to do so [*author's note*: for to do so would lose money and that would not be "rational"]. And as the big established lines knew that they were in a position to provide a service more economically than any newcomer could furnish it they did not fear competition. But the worthy theory failed in the case of the railroads.[4]

J. P. Morgan, of course, went on to earn enormous sums advising railroads how to avoid value-destroying behaviors so that those railroads could responsibly fulfill their obligations to the holders of their securities, many of whom were Morgan's clients.[5] Meanwhile, the economic "school books" moved on to the idea of "bounded rationality," which can be summarized as follows:

> How do managers deal with all the information in front of them? They try to pick out and isolate only that which is important: . . . In other words, we [as human beings] eliminate all apparently irrelevant information, thereby using a subset of all existing information, much of which we won't ever know. [Herbert] Simon called this model "bounded rationality," proposing that decisions are made within a set of constraints, and that the information available to the decision-maker limits his or her rationality. He cannot be omniscient; hence he might not make the best possible choice.[6]

While I do not know Warren Buffett, I doubt the above quote relates to what he meant by the term "rational" when he described Singleton's corporate management behavior. The qualification "doubt" is important because I have been unable to locate a source for how either Buffett, or the late Benjamin Graham, specifically define the terms "rational" and "rationality." I therefore spoke with a well-known Buffett scholar and investor, Robert Hagstrom. During our conversation, he commented on "rationality" in a way that closely followed what he wrote in his book, *Investing: The Last Liberal Art*, namely that "the most common thinking errors have less to do with intelligence and more with rationality—or, more accurately, the lack of it."[7] Upon hearing this, I inquired how he specifically defined the term "rationality." His reply included a reference to the work of Professor Keith Stanovich, who defined this term very practically as "behaving in the world so that you get exactly what you want, given the resources (physical and mental) available to you."[8] This definition logically links strategic (or aspirational) statements with execution (or operational) activities in a way that can be highly insightful. To illustrate how, we will examine the "rationality" of two corporate managers, both of whom declared their intention to create value for their shareholders.

"Irrational" Managerial Behavior

Tracking actual-to-expected performance is a widely followed performance management practice. Such practices tend to be highly tactical and focus on the sales, profit, and growth projections profiled in strategic plans compared to short-term (monthly, quarterly, and annual) performance metrics. However, similar kinds of analyses can be applied more broadly to assess corporate managerial rationality. For example, consider the case of Al Dunlap, who was a controversial corporate manager.

Dunlap's method of operating was to drastically cut the costs of troubled firms, sell off noncore assets to pay down/off debt and then position or otherwise "stage" the new, leaner firm for sale to strategic buyers. His most well-known and successful turnaround was the Scott Paper Company, which was sold in 1995 to Kimberly-Clark for $9.4 billion.[9] Following this deal, on November 18, 1996, Dunlap participated in a panel discussion on "Corporate Responsibilities"; the video is available online from C-SPAN.[10] At approximately the one-hour mark in the video, Dunlap makes the following statement: "I believe that when shareholders give you the money, they want you to come up with new products, new facilities, new ideas, and I believe if you create genuine wealth for the shareholders . . ." This statement will help to form the basis of our forthcoming analysis, but first it is important to note that, in addition to participating in the above panel in 1996, Dunlap was also appointed CEO of Sunbeam.

At the time, Sunbeam was suffering from significant performance issues and its shareholders effectively wanted to replicate

Scott's success,[11] which did not occur. A *Businessweek* article helps to explain why:

> For one thing, Dunlap's celebrity had helped push the stock [of Sunbeam] to premium levels, making it too rich for most acquirers. For another, it was becoming increasingly difficult to meet Dunlap's projections. To double revenues to $2 billion by 1999, Sunbeam would have to increase sales five times faster than rivals. To boost operating margins to 20 percent in just over a year, Sunbeam would have to improve its profitability more than twelvefold from the measly 2.5 percent margins it had. To generate $600 million in sales through new products by 1999, the company would have to smash home runs with every at-bat.
>
> Almost all his executives believed these goals were impractical. Dunlap, however, refused to acknowledge the near-impossibility of meeting them. Instead, he began putting excruciating pressure on those who reported to him, who in turn passed that intimidation down the line. People were told that either they meet their goals or another person would be found to do it for them. Their livelihood hung on making numbers that were not makeable.[12]

Several items profiled above reflect increasing levels of risk at Sunbeam, which the firm's board, financial analysts, and more active shareholders could have been mindful of. First is the price appreciation caused by "Dunlap's celebrity." Premium price levels are difficult to sustain and therefore are indicative of strategic and investment risk.[13] Also, as Benjamin Graham and David Dodd insightfully observed, creating shareholder value includes an "obligation" by corporate managers to prevent "either absurdly high or unduly low prices for their securities."[14] But this is not what occurred at Sunbeam. Rather than caution against excessive market valuation, Dunlap implemented aggressive "stretch goals," presumably to rationalize and enhance the market valuation, and he exerted significant pressure on his employees to meet those goals.

As the drive to achieve the stretch goals progressed, it led to gaming behavior. Per the previously quoted *Businessweek* article, "In an effort to hang on to their jobs and their [stock] options, some Sunbeam managers began all sorts of game playing. Commissions were withheld from independent sales reps. Bills went unpaid. Some vendors were forced to accept partial payment. One director reported getting a call from a headhunter begging for help in collecting a bill from Sunbeam." In can be argued that behavior like this was not only well within the realm of possibility but was indeed "rational." To explain why, consider that if Sunbeam managers did not meet their stretch goals they would lose their jobs with near 100 percent certainty, but if they gamed the system and met their goals, they might not lose their jobs; hence, it was rational, albeit unethical, for them to game the system. Clearly, this state of affairs was not, and is not, consistent with value creation.[15]

When the risk of deviant behavior such as performance gaming is not mitigated, it can become "normalized," whereby such behavior incrementally increases until it reaches a tipping point.[16] This appears to have happened at Sunbeam because its gaming behavior seems to have spilled over into accounting:

As Sunbeam moved toward the holiday season, its struggle to make its numbers became more desperate. Of all the ploys, few were as controversial and daring as the "bill-and-hold" sales of barbecue grills the company began making in early November. Anxious to extend the selling season for the product and boost sales in Dunlap's "turnaround year," the company offered retailers major discounts to buy grills nearly six months before they were needed. The retailers did not have to pay for the grills or accept delivery of them for six months. The downside was evident: The company was booking what would have been future sales in the present. Indeed, after Dunlap's departure from the company, outside auditors would force a restatement of

Sunbeam's financials, pushing most of these sales—$62 million worth—into future quarters.[17]

A great deal can be said about the above quote, especially that it is obviously not consistent with Dunlap's earlier statements about creating shareholder value during his participation on the panel; in other words, his decisions and behaviors at Sunbeam did not involve the creation of new products, new facilities, new ideas, or "genuine wealth." Therefore, those decisions and behaviors were irrational per Professor Stanovich's definition. Significantly, the term "irrational" is used here not simply as a descriptor but as a leading indicator of business risks that were observable in real time and thus could have been closely monitored and acted on by the firm's board, financial analysts, and more active shareholders.

"Rational" Managerial Behavior

Consider now the example of the late Henry Singleton, who was profiled in the last chapter. In 1986, which was toward the end of his career, Singleton spun off Teledyne's Argonaut Insurance Group for $234 million, which equated to a gain of 169 percent based on the 1969 acquisition price. After Singleton spun off the rest of Teledyne's insurance companies in 1990, journalist Eric Savitz made this observation:

Spin-offs, of course, are now familiar on Wall Street, but what makes this one a little different is that it represents another in a long series of moves by Singleton to enrich his shareholders. While other companies spend a lot of time talking about "maximizing shareholder value," Singleton's company has a history of doing just that. As noted in a profile of the company in *Barron's* last December, Teledyne, over the years, has repeatedly repurchased its stock, lifted its dividend and spun off profitable subsidiaries, all of which have appreciably benefited shareholders.[18]

Throughout his career, Singleton's actions were extremely consistent with his communicated goals, objectives, and statements; thus, it could reasonably be stated that, per Professor Stanovich's definition, his decisions and behaviors were indeed "100 percent rational," as Warren Buffett observed. Indeed, I believe this is consistent with how Buffett—and Graham before him—define "rationality," but that is just my opinion. Much more important is Singleton's track record of rational behavior that was clearly observable in real time, assuming investors and business partners were looking for it.

Practical Applications

The historical cases of Al Dunlap and Henry Singleton are extreme examples and therefore useful for illustration purposes. In practice, few corporate (and investment) managers are either "100 percent rational" or completely irrational. Therefore, some people could argue that while "rationality" may be an interesting research topic, it has limited practical value. But I believe they are mistaken. To the extent investments are made in going concerns, those investments have a greater chance of being profitable if they are made in firms led by corporate managers who have a track record of delivering performance consistent with their stated goals and objectives over time, assuming those goals and objectives lead to sustainable profitability, increased productivity, and/ or growth—subject, of course, to the prices at which such investments are made.[19]

Following this line of thinking, one way to identify potential value creating investments is to rationalize corporate performance with publicly communicated goals, objectives, and strategies over time.

For example, during one firm's M&A deliberations, intense focus was directed to evaluating a target's asking price, which was very high but nevertheless consistent with private market valuations at the time. To enhance the analysis, we compared the target to its peer group in terms of the consistency with which the performance of each firm rationalized to the public statements of its corporate managers over time. Results of this analysis are not available for publication, but the target in this case scored lower than its peers, thereby suggesting potential value realization issues that possibly warranted a lower valuation. While issues like this one may have been discovered during due diligence, the fact that we actively looked for them guided by rationality-inspired information enabled a much more insightful analysis, which ultimately resulted in a lower bid than a traditional private market valuation suggested.[20]

An enabler of this kind of analysis is clear and candid executive communications. Identifying such communications is highly qualitative and can require significant amounts of time to both collect and analyze. To facilitate it, L. J. Rittenhouse publishes a "CEO Candor & Culture Survey" that lists the top and bottom firms from candor and communication-related perspectives.[21] Information like this is highly actionable; for example, consider firms toward the top of lists like this one, which could present lucrative investment or M&A opportunities if pricing is attractive. Additionally, the change in candor rankings year-over-year could also help to inform investment/M&A analyses. To the extent a firm's candor rankings are improving along with their performance, greater confidence could be placed in the corporate managers to achieve their stated goals and objectives in a timely manner to close any identified "value gap."[22] Furthermore, this information can also be used to determine if investors should become active in certain investments. For example, value investor Michael Price has stated that while he does not start out active, he will become active when boards and managements of the firms he invests in do "things that are not in the interest of long-term shareholders."[23] Active trigger points could be informed by, for instance, a negative change in a firm's candor rankings or performance that is increasingly inconsistent with a firm's public statements.

Conclusion

This chapter profiled four ways rationality–based or inspired insights can practically inform strategic and investment analyses. Each flowed from the basic definition that rational decisions and actions are those that are consistent with the goals, objectives, and statements that preceded the decisions and actions over time:

- Disconnects between corporate managers' goals, objectives, and statements and their decisions and actions are indicative of increasing levels of business risk. This behavior was observed at Sunbeam, and resulted in the destruction of significant value. More recently, James Grant made a similar analysis when he compared the words that Restoration Hardware's "irrepressible chairman and CEO, Gary Friedman, might say, with the words he has already spoken and with the deeds the company has already performed and may perform in the future. Our predisposition is bearish."[24] The company's stock price on December 8, 2015, which is presumably when Grant's analysis went to press, was quoted at $92.34/share.[25] On December 14, 2015, Google Finance quoted it at $78.65/share, a decline of nearly 15 percent. (The stock bottomed out at $25.99 on June 17, 2016, per the same source, and then went on to recover powerfully.)
- Corporate managers who candidly communicate their intention to create value *and* who have a history of doing so over time—such as the late Henry Singleton—offer lucrative investment or M&A opportunities when their firms' securities are favorably priced, such as during periods of

general market distress and periods of expanding market volatility.

- Comparing the rationality of a firm's corporate managers with those of its peer group over time can help to provide context to relative valuations, which can supplement other forms of investment, M&A, and risk management analyses.

- "Candor scores" could be useful investment/M&A screening aids; for example, the reasonably priced securities of a firm with a high candor ranking (especially over time) could present a lucrative investment/M&A opportunity. Such scores could also serve as potential risk management screens. For example, the securities of a firm with falling candor scores (especially after a prolonged price run-up) or performance that is increasingly inconsistent with external communications could be indicative of increased levels of business risk, thereby warranting more active investment management.

There are many other uses of rationality–based/inspired analysis including the following, which will conclude this chapter. Warren Buffett once observed, "To invest successfully over a lifetime does not require a stratospheric IQ, unusual business insights, or inside information. What's needed is a sound intellectual framework for making decisions and the ability to keep emotions from corroding that framework."[26] The concept of rationality can enable both aspects of this observation. First, anchoring an analytical framework to rational corporate management is a practical way of narrowing the investment/M&A universe down to the best-managed firms, thereby helping to mitigate investment risk. And second, making a concerted effort to invest/allocate capital rationally, or consistent with your goals, objectives, and statements, will help to prevent emotions from corroding your framework. To the extent corporate and investment managers can accomplish this over time, they will be well placed to capitalize on the irrational behavior of others in the modern, highly uncertain capital markets that tend to be characterized by a wide variety of information asymmetries. Such managers should be able to overcome "the main obstacles" of investment analysis that were observed by Benjamin Graham and David Dodd in the first quote that introduced this chapter.

7

Corporate Management and "Modern Security Analysis"

"Brilliant management in one context is not necessarily brilliant management in another; those who are good deal makers at one time may be bad in another period. A talent for operational efficiency, for example, may obscure a predilection for misunderstanding sophisticated finance."
—MARTIN J. WHITMAN AND MARTIN SHUBIK[1]

"Deals are not like a chess game, where by definition if one side wins, the other loses; they are not zero sum. A well-structured deal has something in it for everyone."
—MARTIN J. WHITMAN AND FERNANDO DIZ[2]

MARTIN J. WHITMAN passed away on April 16, 2018, which marked the end of an era.[3] I had the opportunity to work with him in the preparation of the paper that preceded this chapter, which spoke to the evolution of managerial skills given current marketplace dynamics and demands. For example, historical levels of volatility and governmental intervention during and after the 2007–2008 financial crisis caused many people to reexamine long-standing economic beliefs, starting with "the world's dumbest idea," maximizing shareholder value.[4] This is not, of course, meant to suggest that the price of a firm's stock is not important. Instead, it is meant to direct attention to the dichotomy inherent in modern shareholder value theory; namely, even though value is inherently subjective, a belief has emerged that daily market pricing is "the" measure of value and that as a result, earnings must be tightly managed over the short term so as not to disappoint "the market." This is nonsense, but when markets are booming few bother to question the premises underlying the boom until the inevitable bust occurs.

Contrary to many of today's micro/short-term-oriented investors, professional value investors tend to be focused on the longer term, and this carries over to the corporate managers of the firms many have chosen to invest in, such as Warren Buffett of Berkshire Hathaway, the Tisch family of Loews, and John Malone, who led Liberty Media, Liberty Global, and Qurate Retail Group (formerly known as Liberty Interactive), to name just three well-known examples.

To help explain the skills evolution beyond current practices, Whitman and Fernando Diz wrote *Modern Security Analysis*. Here are some of the insights from that book that I felt were particularly significant to corporate management.

Creditworthiness Rather than Earnings

Whitman and Diz focus on creditworthiness instead of "shareholder value," which can be both highly transitory and subject to micro/short- to mid-term volatility. Among other things, such a focus "affords management options to be opportunistic; that is, use [their superior financial position] as an asset in resource conversion activities to create wealth."[5] More on this later, but first it is important to understand that Whitman and Diz do not employ either a credit rating or a value-at-risk (or VaR)–derived measure to evaluate creditworthiness; rather, they define "creditworthiness or credit capacity [as] a function of three factors: (1) the amount of debt, (2) the terms of debt, and (3) the productivity in the use of proceeds arising out of the borrowings,"[6] all assessed via rigorous bottom-up analysis. The implications of this definition are significant.

First, while "the amount of debt" may seem relatively simple to understand, in practice it is often not well understood, for both theoretical and practical reasons. Theoretically, academic economists believe that capital structure is irrelevant.[7] While many corporate managers snicker at the silliness of this "proposition," the fact remains that during the financial crisis of 2007–2008 many corporate managers "didn't know their own balance sheets."[8] As a result, they either became forced sellers or were so impaired by the volatility of the crisis that they were not able to take advantage of the distressed investment/M&A opportunities that were generated by the crisis. Contrast these managers with, for example, Warren Buffett and the lucrative distressed investments he made during the crisis in Goldman Sachs and General Electric. He was able to strategically deploy his superior financial position during the crisis, which resulted in the creation of significant wealth, in contrast to so many other corporate managers who were financially impaired at the time.[9]

Next, consider "the terms of debt." Again, this may sound relatively simple to understand, but we know from recent experience that in practice there is nothing simple about it. For example, consider the Credit Support Annexes (which include collateral requirements) to various credit default swaps that AIG contracted to, which contributed to their failure during the 2007–2008 financial crisis. The risks posed by these Annexes were either not understood or ignored by AIG management prior to the crisis.[10]

Last, but certainly not least, is the productive use of financial resources, which is an activity that some corporate managers struggle with. For example, a question I am asked by some managers interested in applying value investing principles to corporate finance goes something like this: "This all looks great in a case study, but how will I *know* that an asset or distressed deal is favorably priced and right for me to buy?" Whitman and Diz provide a practical answer, but first some historical context.

One technique that Benjamin Graham developed and employed with great success was purchasing securities at prices less than *net-net value*, which is calculated as current assets less **total** liabilities.

Over time, net-net based opportunities have become increasingly scarce. The net-net concept, however, remains strategically intriguing: buying the proverbial dollar of highly liquid assets for pennies. Therefore, Whitman and Diz modified the concept for modern use by basing their analysis on replacement cost values instead of simply following GAAP accounting, which allows them to extend the asset scope beyond GAAP-defined current assets, as the following example illustrates:

> Under Section 1231 of the U.S. Internal Revenue Code, the sale at a loss of [property, plant and equipment] used in a trade or business usually gives rise to an ordinary loss for income tax purposes. In that case, a corporation may be able to apply the loss first to reduce current year taxes and any excess loss might be used to get quickie cash refunds from the IRS with regard to taxes paid in the prior two years.[11]

To close this section, it is important to note the ethical element that differentiates creditworthiness from shareholder value. Modern shareholder value theory has resulted in an almost "anything goes," zero-sum environment that is not conducive to either long-term wealth creation or, for that matter, broader stakeholder (customers, employees, regulators, etc.) well-being. Creditworthiness, on the other hand, is inherently character based, which is something that has generally been forgotten, and therefore, "It is important to remember that the word credit comes from the [Latin] word *credere*, which means 'to believe.'"[12] And as value investor Seth Klarman observed, "A promise is only as good as the entity making it."[13] This indisputable fact led the late J. P. Morgan to famously state the following in his testimony before the Pujo Committee in 1912:

QUESTION: Is not commercial credit based primarily upon money or property?
J. P. MORGAN: No, sir, the first thing is character.

QUESTION: Before money or property?

J. P. MORGAN: Before money or anything else. Money cannot buy it. . . . Because a man I do not trust could not get money from me on all the bonds in Christendom.[14]

Sometimes moving forward requires relearning the lessons of the past. However, this is not to say that creditworthiness is a perfect measure. Given the subjective nature of value,[15] and the inherent uncertainty of the future, there are *no* perfect measures. Nevertheless, creditworthiness that is assessed via rigorous bottom-up analysis is a much better, and more insightful, way to evaluate and manage a business over time (or in the long term) compared to the management of quarterly earnings (or cash flows) and the movement of a stock's price.

Corporate Managers as Operators, Investors, and Financiers

Many corporate managers consider themselves operators, and for good reason: it is how many of them came up through the ranks and were educated. As a result, many firms have traditional Corporate Development departments that tend to function on the same processes and techniques as just about every other Corporate Development department. Perhaps this is a reason why so many corporate mergers and acquisitions fail, and why the failures seem to be caused for many of the same reasons.[16] For example, the major reason M&A deals fail is that "the company doing the buying overpays."[17] While overpaying may not have many consequences when financial markets are booming, it can have significant consequences when booms end, as all booms do. For example, it is increasingly understood that corporate managers can no longer be guided by an operational philosophy like this one: "When the music stops, in terms of liquidity, things will be complicated. But as long as the music is playing, you've got to get up and dance. We're still dancing."[18,19]

Whitman and Diz implicitly grasp that the days of growing out of a bad deal, or a series of bad deals, seem to be coming to an end; as a result, corporate managers in general will have to demonstrate much greater levels of expertise in the areas of investing/corporate development and capital markets access/financing than they have in the past. The key enabler of such capabilities is the attainment of an information/analytical advantage in the industries they operate in;[20] in other words, they need to use "the available information in a superior manner."[21]

Investing and financing expertise does not only pertain to the acquisition of new assets; it also pertains to the conversion of existing assets into more productive uses, which is formally known as *resource conversion*.[22] When executed by skilled corporate managers such activities can be strategically significant, as illustrated below:

> In 2012, it seemed most hostile takeovers were initiated by distressed investors who acquired credits in troubled companies and then in a Chapter 11 reorganization received common stock for their credits as part of a plan of reorganization.[23] This is the way Brookfield Asset Management obtained control of General Growth Properties in 2011; how John Paulson obtained control of certain resort hotels; and how Cavco Industries in partnership with Third Avenue Value Fund obtained control of Palm Harbor Homes in 2011.[24]

Given the dynamics of today's marketplace, resource conversions could intensify and become much more commonplace in the future.

Understanding the Motivations and Practices of Activists

Activist investors receive a great deal of attention, as they tend to generate significant levels of managerial pressure and publicity. Like all activities, however, "activist investing" is context-dependent: if it is applied to poor or fraudulent managements, it can be very beneficial, but if it is applied to strong or sound managements, it can be disruptive. Regardless of a specific application, however, there is much that corporate managers can learn from the discipline of activist investing as Whitman and Diz explain in *Modern Security Analysis:*

- The Economics of Private Equity Leveraged Buyouts—"The ability to market unsecured debt reflects super-attractive access to capital markets."[25]
- The Use of Creative Finance in a Corporate Takeover—"The [Reliance Insurance Company] case is of interest in part because of the extremely attractive consideration that was given to providers of cash so that they obtained (a) a safe, above-average return on a tax-privileged basis as well as (b) an opportunity to participate in potential market appreciation."[26]
- The Use of Creative Finance to Benefit Controlling Stockholders—"Deals are not like a chess game, where by definition if one side wins, the other loses; they are not zero sum. A well-structured deal has something in it for everyone."[27]

In closing, it is important to understand that the subjects described above—(a) creditworthiness, (b) executives as operators, investors, and financiers, and (c) understanding the motivation and practices of activists—need to be performed simultaneously. In fact, when you consider the insights that can be derived from the interactions of these activities over time, you can begin to more fully appreciate the accomplishments of corporate managers such as Warren Buffett, the Tisch family, and John Malone, as well as the potential of future corporate managers who are able to follow their example. To help facilitate this, I interviewed Marty Whitman a few years before his death during the preparation of the paper that preceded this chapter.

Question: In your long and successful career as a value investor, do you have any thoughts how corporate managers can strategically approach inefficient markets?

Answer: It is important to understand that most markets are inefficient as a consequence of the analyses that are employed in those markets. For example, the following characteristics are typical of conventional market analyses that many investors, analysts, and corporate managers employ, none of which facilitate long-term wealth creation: short-term focus; top-down oriented; centered on the periodic income account to the exclusion of the balance sheet and financial position considerations; fundamental assumptions of price equilibria, a consequence of which is a focus on "outlooks" instead of underlying values and value drivers. Such characteristics tend to negate the efficient appraisal, and management, of corporations with a perpetual life and the securities they issue.[28]

Successful corporate managers of the past like Henry Singleton and Larry Tisch viewed market prices not as "efficient," but rather as something to watch and take advantage of when the time was right. Market prices certainly were (and are) not something to worry about or micro-manage. The practical implications of this are significant; for example, distressed credit prices signal the existence of potentially bargain assets. In such cases, the focus of analysis is neither on price volatility nor on correlation, which are important statistics of efficient market–based [i.e., academic] finance, but rather on whether the credit will be performing or non-performing over time; and if non-performing, whether adequate collateral exists to secure it. The actions stemming from the analytical differences of these two approaches can be quite dramatic, and often differentiate a successful corporate manager from unsuccessful ones. The earlier example of Warren Buffett and his distress investments in Goldman Sachs and General Electric is a case in point.

Question: Can you describe how corporate managers could access capital markets more strategically?

Answer: One consequence of inefficient markets is that capital markets access is highly period specific: At certain times, the markets seem to almost give money away such as during the dot.com boom,[29] with the Facebook IPO and now with Alibaba.[30,31] In such cases, it is more economical to fund operations through the capital markets than retained earnings. However, at other times, the markets can freeze causing widespread liquidity disruption such as during 2008. At times like this, retained earnings are much more economical than the capital markets. Therefore, corporate managers should not employ fixed funding models; instead, funding models should be flexible over time so that corporate managers can take advantage of short-term market inefficiencies as they arise.

There is an element of timing involved in this, of course, but corporate managers skilled in *fundamental finance* who operate with long-term time horizons have been able to successfully negotiate it.[32] For example, consider Henry Singleton: in 1980, he substituted the undervalued equity of Teledyne for favorably priced debt, and in so doing effectively "called" or estimated the top of the bond market. For a more recent example, our book analyzes in detail the 2005 acquisition of Hertz Global Holdings by Clayton, Dubilier & Rice, Carlyle Group, and ML Global Private Equity Fund.[33]

Question: Many firms are implementing risk management programs to manage their firm's risk profiles from the top down. Do you have any advice for the executives of these firms?

Answer: As we note in our book, "In fundamental finance, the word *risk* is always modified by an adjective. There is no general risk.

There is market risk, investment risk, interest rate risk, inflation risk, failure to meet maturities risk, securities fraud risk, excessive promoters' compensation risk, and so on."[34] The two risks most corporate managers focus on are market risk (price fluctuations) and investment risk (problems with the business), and of the two investment risk is by far the most important.[35]

Investment risk is best managed via rigorous bottom-up analysis because such analysis is inherently management-oriented. For example, successful investment risk management typically results in:

- A strong financial position; meaning, the relative absence of liabilities (on-balance sheet, off-balance sheet, and "out there in the world"), the existence of valuable assets such as cash or near cash, and free cash flows from operations;
- A reasonably well–managed business; and
- An understandable business, which almost always means comprehensible disclosures and audited financial statements, with the possible exceptions of the common stocks of high tech start-ups and companies involved with natural resource discoveries.[36]

One benefit of this kind of risk management approach is that it facilitates the identification of strategic opportunities when market risk and investment risk profiles diverge. For example, in our book we discuss the case of Kmart in 1995: despite rising levels of market risk (via increasing levels of price volatility) at the time, the firm's credits seemed to generate little-to-no investment risk. This divergence resulted in a lucrative, low-risk distress investment opportunity.[37]

Question: On the subject of investment opportunities, what advice do you have for corporate managers who are interested in employing your techniques in their Corporate Development functions?

Answer: Certain corporate managers can, and do, create wealth through opportunistic investing/M&A, where opportunistic is often a function of superior financial position. However, and as noted above, M&A mistakes can be rather common.[38] One way to mitigate M&A risk is to focus on how potential deals can help a firm over time, which bottom-up analysis can powerfully enable. For example, consider the historic 1968 acquisition of Reliance Insurance Company by Leasco, which we analyze in our book.[39] In essence, this deal created tremendous wealth due to its creative financing, the accounting treatment it employed, and "because it enabled Leasco to tie up key blocks of common stock without risking cash, unless it was to obtain control of Reliance."[40]

For another example, consider how taxation can powerfully impact the economics of a deal over time, which is something that not all corporate managers adequately appreciate. For instance, contrast the example of John Malone, whose approach to taxes was always intensely strategic,[41] with the way that AT&T virtually ignored the tax consequences of its 1998 acquisition of Malone's TCI.[42]

8

Value Realization Is "The Most Important Thing"

"We must inquire, first, 'What are the factors which will contribute most directly to an increase in value?' And second, 'What are the prospects of these factors being realized in the near future?'"

—BENJAMIN GRAHAM[1]

"Even a promising net-net investment can be doomed if the company's assets are squandered on money-losing operations or unwise acquisitions."

—HOWARD MARKS[2]

IN THIS CHAPTER, we move on to the subject of value realization, which is important because *all* strategic initiatives are contingent on some event or sequence of events to realize value. There are three general ways investors manage this contingency. First, they passively monitor developments and wait for the market to bid prices higher. Second, they can become active by pushing for decisions intended to realize value over time.[3] Lastly, they can acquire an asset outright and take actions to realize value themselves. Corporate managers tend to focus on the last option but all three are important; for example, when a firm buys securities, it may passively monitor the market pricing of its investments, but when it acquires a firm or business unit it may become active in its operations if performance suffers. Therefore, an understanding of value realization in general helps increase the probability of successful strategic initiatives over time.

In 2011, Howard Marks published *The Most Important Thing.*[4] Marks is the cofounder and chairman of Oaktree Capital Management in Los Angeles, California, which is a fund specializing in credit–based value investments. Upon reading his book, and attending his presentation at the New York Society of Security Analysts,[5] I was struck by how much of the material was broadly applicable to corporate management, especially from a value realization perspective, which is profiled in this chapter and will conclude **Part 1** of this book.

Corporate Strategy

If economics is the darling of the social sciences, then strategy is the darling of business/corporate management literature.[6] Innumerable books, journals, and articles have been written on the subject of strategy, and yet it generally remains elusive for many corporate managers and investors. At the core of every successful strategy, however, is some form of differentiation. The reason for this is straightforward, as Marks explains:

> Since other [competitors] may be smart, well informed and highly computerized, you must find an edge they don't have. You must think of something they haven't thought of, see things they miss or bring insight they don't possess. You have to react differently and behave differently. In short, being right may be a necessary condition for investment success, but it won't be sufficient. You must be more right than others . . . which by definition means your thinking has to be different.[7]

The concept of differentiation runs throughout *The Most Important Thing* because many of the most successful strategies/ investments are differentiated from the beginning of their life cycle. Consider that "Many of the best bargains at any point in time are found among the things other investors can't or won't do."[8] To capitalize on such bargains, corporate managers/investors must "have an edge in either information or analysis, or both."[9] Employing an edge to consistently operate against market perceptions is extremely difficult,[10] but one indication it is being accomplished is that there is no—or at best little—competition for an asset. If there is competition, it could mean the asset is viewed optimistically and thus priced higher, and according to Marks, "it takes a lot of hard work or a lot of luck to turn something bought at a too-high price into a successful investment."[11]

The above activities are not frequently addressed in mainstream strategy research even though they are differentiation–based. That research does, however, focus heavily on value proposition differentiation, which is the defining characteristic of all *franchises* or firms operating with sustainable competitive advantages, which generally center on either product/service differentiation or being the low-cost provider of more commodity-like products/services. Franchises generate returns greater than those required, and thus they tend to attract competition that erodes their advantages, and hence returns, over time. However, endogenous reasons could also erode a competitive advantage. As Marks correctly observed, "Most people seem to think outstanding performance to date presages outstanding future performance. Actually, it's more likely that outstanding performance to date has borrowed from the future and thus presages subpar performance from here on out."[12] Managing capital structure (or financing) is one aspect of value realization; others are discussed below.

Corporate Management

Effective corporate managers actively mitigate the risk of value destruction, which is important considering how often value is destroyed. For example, Marks observed, "It's remarkable how many leading competitors from [Oaktree Capital Management's] early years as investors are no longer leading competitors (or competitors at all). While a number faltered because of flaws in their organization or business model, others disappeared because they insisted on pursuing high returns in low-return environments."[13] The managerial aspects of each of these failure sources are discussed below.

Managing a business model is critically important because many business failures are caused by "organizational flaws [that] rendered their game plans unsustainable."[14] If, as Robert S. Kaplan and David P. Norton state, "The art of leadership is to delicately balance [the] tension between stability and change,"[15] then a business model is the vehicle with which to manage that tension. There are two general ways this can be accomplished.

First, corporate managers can continuously stretch their business model to reach for ever higher performance goals. The thought process behind this approach is that unit managers may propose easily attainable targets, and therefore corporate managers must "stretch" them to realize value, which is defined as a return exceeding that which is required. According to one former corporate manager who employed this approach, "We have found that by reaching for what appears to be the impossible, we often actually do the impossible; and even when we don't quite make it, we inevitably wind up doing much better than we would have done."[16]

An alternative to stretch goals is to intensely manage strategically focused performance with the objective of sustaining, and perhaps extending, a competitive advantage over time, which can, at times, equate to holding performance targets constant. For example, while commenting on GEICO's performance in Berkshire Hathaway's 1996 annual report, Warren Buffett noted, "We never greet good work by raising the bar. If GEICO's performance continues to improve, we will happily keep on making larger [performance] charts."[17] Positives and negatives of this approach, according to Marks, are that "you may hit fewer home runs than another [competitor] . . . but you're also likely to have fewer strikeouts and fewer inning-ending double plays."[18]

Which approach should corporate managers employ to increase the probability of value realization? It depends on the strategy being executed:

- During a turnaround situation, managers should generally stretch their organizations to improve performance before more drastic measures, such as filing for bankruptcy, may be required.
- For adequately performing firms, however, stretching should be employed selectively. The reason for this is that the graveyard of firms that stretched their way to failure (for example, ones that "insisted on pursuing high returns in low return environments") is both wide and deep. Persistent stretching often evolves into persistent fire drills, which over time can stress a business model. And like any structure, business models subject to persistent stress will eventually fracture. Significantly, such fractures may not occur all of a sudden; rather, some business models can incrementally descend into failure, which occurs over time through the gradual loosening of strategic, investment, and/or product standards that cumulatively increase the risk of failure.[19]

Irrespective of which approach is ultimately selected, a key corporate management activity is to mitigate the risk of failure.

Risk

Risk is another area that has been covered by innumerable books, journals, articles, and speeches, much of which focus on models/modeling to quantify the extent of potential future losses. However, as Marks observed, "You can't know the future; you don't have to know the future; and [therefore] the proper goal is to do the best possible job of investing in the absence of that knowledge."[20] A fundamental step in this process is simply "keeping things from going wrong,"[21] which can be accomplished by carefully defining risk and then determining how it should be managed.

First, Marks notes that risk—like value—is inherently subjective and therefore "the risk that matters most is the risk of permanent loss."[22] Not many would argue with either of these statements, but he uses them to argue, contrary to financial orthodoxy, that *high risk cannot be equated with higher returns* because "if riskier investments reliably produced higher returns, they wouldn't be riskier."[23] Consequently, it is the risk of permanent loss from "things going wrong" that must be intensely managed. Value investors manage this risk by buying at discounts to estimated value, which provides them with a margin of safety. As Benjamin Graham explained, "The margin of safety is always dependent on the price paid. It will be large at one price, small at some higher price, nonexistent at some still higher price. . . . It is available for absorbing the effect of miscalculations or worse than average luck."[24]

One way to find margin of safety–based opportunities is to trade with *forced sellers*, or investors and firms under pressure to divest because of some form of distress. As Marks observed, "Since buying from a forced seller is the best thing in the world, *being* a forced seller is the worst. That means it's essential to arrange your affairs so you'll be able to hold on—and not sell—at the worst of times."[25] Viewed in this light, managing risk becomes less a matter of forecasting the future than conservatively assessing the present. A key activity in this effort is estimating where current market conditions are in the context of the overall cycle, which Marks breaks down as follows:

- *The three stages of a bull market:*

  ○ The first, when a few forward-looking people begin to believe things will get better;

- The second, when most investors realize improvement is actually taking place; and
- The third, when everyone concludes things will get better forever.[26]

- *The three stages of a bear market:*

  - The first, when just a few thoughtful investors recognize that, despite the prevailing bullishness, things won't always be rosy;
  - The second, when most investors recognize things are deteriorating; and
  - The third, when everyone's convinced things can only get worse.[27]

To demonstrate how an appreciation for market cycles could have been used in a strategic context, consider the global economy in 2005 and 2006. At that time, many, if not most, investors felt that things would "get better forever" (bull market, stage three). Because *nothing* gets better forever, investors conservatively assessing cyclical activity at the time could have strategically positioned their portfolios to first survive an impending market turn and then capitalize on the forced sales that characterize such turns. Marks describes his experiences doing exactly that during the 2007–2009 financial crisis:

> A full meltdown of the world financial system was considered possible; in fact, the first steps—the bankruptcy of Lehman Brothers and the absorption or rescue of Bear Sterns, Merrill Lynch, AIG, Fannie Mae, Freddie Mac, Wachovia and WaMu—had taken place. Since this was the biggest crisis ever, investors bought into the third stage [of a bear market], during which "everyone's convinced things can only get worse," more than ever. Thus, in many asset classes, the things determined by the pendulum's swing—the price declines in 2008, the resultant

investment opportunities at the nadir, and the gains in 2009—
were the greatest I've ever seen.[28]

For another example, consider that as the cycle developed in
2005 and 2006, the price of risk management instruments fell to
margin of safety–rich levels, which offered economical hedging
opportunities analogous to "cheap insurance" that several astute
investors capitalized on thereby enabling them to profit during the
2007–2008 financial crisis (bear market, stages two and three).

The point of the above examples is not to retrospectively pick
cases that "fit the facts," but rather to demonstrate how a conservative assessment of the present can be incorporated with the margin
of safety principle to facilitate high-probability value-realization
activities across market cycles.

PART 2
Practice

WE NOW MOVE from theory to practice, specifically to three case studies that practically demonstrate value realization in action. Each of the following cases deals with a different facet of value realization, which is accomplished in a manner consistent with the theory profiled in **Part 1**:

- **Chapter 9** profiles the GEICO case and illustrates how significant value was realized following a growth–based acquisition;
- **Chapter 10** profiles the GTI case and how analytical output was used to powerfully realize value in a corporate turnaround; and
- **Chapter 11** profiles the Union Pacific case and how value was realized following a significant macroeconomic disruption without any kind of macroeconomic intervention.

A word on how and why these cases were selected. First, I selected historical rather than contemporary case studies to ensure that the findings of each case were, in fact, "the findings." I do not want to run the risk of profiling a case in this book that turns out to be fallacious (such as, for example, the profile of Fannie Mae in the book *Good to Great*, which was mentioned earlier).

Second, the cases were chosen to illustrate a particular aspect of value realization that I have personally been questioned about by a corporate manager. In the case of GEICO, after my first book was published, which included a valuation of the GEICO acquisition, I received a great deal of inquiries from corporate (and investment) managers that went something like this: "Okay, we get GEICO, we've always gotten GEICO. The question is, how will we 'know' when the next GEICO comes around? And how will we 'know' management will be capable of realizing value like the management at GEICO did?" **Chapter 9** provides actionable answers to questions like these.

A great deal has been written on the subject of "analytics," but virtually none of it pertains to how quantitative output can be practically operationalized to achieve a strategic objective. To address this issue, **Chapter 10** profiles the use of a relatively simple financial distress model, which was used to realize value in a corporate turnaround. Significantly, the lessons of the case are not limited to either turnarounds or even financial models. They are broad-based.

Chapter 11 profiles how value was realized following a major economic disruption without any kind of governmental assistance, including via monetary policy. This case is the capstone of the book for several reasons. First, it demonstrates many of the concepts discussed in this book in a holistic and practical way. Second, it shows that effective corporate management can successfully navigate severe macroeconomic disruption without the need for government intervention, which is a lesson that very much needs to be learned today. Like many people, I was both shocked and sickened by all of the bailouts and easy money policies that followed the 2007–2008 financial crisis. Lastly, this chapter sheds light on the positive exploits of a historical figure who has been much maligned, including by business and financial historians who, frankly, should know better.

As previously noted, each chapter is somewhat technical and should be approached as such. In other words, while the first part of the book is meant to be a fairly quick and easy read, the second part will likely take some time to get through. Following the cases, the book will close with a **Conclusion.**

9

Value Realization at GEICO

"The 'bargain issues' were practically all restricted to the purchase of common stocks at less than two-thirds of their net-current-asset value. Remarkably few final losses were shown in this category, comprising the purchase of many hundred such issues over a period of more than thirty years. However, it is both paradoxical and typical of financial experience generally that the most profitable Graham-Newman operation of all did not meet this exacting requirement. This was the purchase of a 50 percent ownership of Government Employees Insurance Company [GEICO] at a price only slightly below its asset value."
—BENJAMIN GRAHAM[1]

"The key to investing is not assessing how much an industry is going to affect society, or how much it will grow, but rather determining the competitive advantage of any given company and, above all, the durability of that advantage. The products or services that have wide, sustainable moats around them are the ones that deliver rewards to investors."
—WARREN E. BUFFETT[2]

CORPORATE STRATEGY in the 1960s and 1970s often included a form of portfolio analysis that,[3] on several occasions, resulted in the divestiture of underperforming units.[4] Investments in these units were, at times, analogous to what Benjamin Graham called "cigar butts," or firms down on their luck "that had a couple of puffs [of] smoke left in them" so that, with cost cutting and moderate performance improvement, the deals frequently resulted in profitable investments. So profitable have these investments been, in fact, that competition for similar deals has grown intense, making them increasingly scarce. A potential alternative to this form of investment could exist in growth–based franchises.

A *franchise* is value investing nomenclature for a firm operating with a sustainable competitive advantage, which consistently generates returns in excess of those required. A growth–based franchise opportunity exists when a growing franchise can be acquired at a reasonable margin of safety. Realizing value on this form of investment is heavily dependent on the quality of management; in the right hands, growth–based franchise deals can be extremely profitable investments, as Warren Buffett's 1995 acquisition of GEICO illustrates.

This chapter presents an approach for identifying, evaluating, and tracking the value realization of growth–based franchise opportunities in the context of the GEICO case. The scope of the approach is necessarily wide since it covers multiple activities and is therefore multi-disciplinary, incorporating financial, strategic, and operational considerations. The theme of franchise (or a firm operating with a sustainable competitive advantage) ties the concepts together into a unified, practical approach that can be used to realize value across industries. Before presenting the approach, we will put the GEICO acquisition in context by providing a brief overview of its operating history up to the time Buffett acquired it.

GEICO

GEICO was founded in 1936 by the late Leo Godwin, Sr. According to a popular account, "he believed that 'if he lowered costs in the company by marketing directly to carefully targeted customer groups, he'd be able to pass along lower premiums and still earn a profit.' With his wife, Lillian, he worked twelve hours a day for little or no salary for several years to implement his business dream. In 1940, after operating in the red for several years, the company realized its first profit. In 1948, GEICO became publicly owned. . . ."[5] Godwin's strategy, in short, was to offer automobile insurance directly to governmental employees, and later to other drivers deemed relatively "safe," instead of through traditional insurance agents which, in conjunction with low operating costs, would allow GEICO to compete economically in its targeted market. Implementing this strategy produced significant performance over time; for example, by 1975, GEICO was the country's fourth-largest automobile insurance company with a 4 percent market share.[6]

However, in the mid-1970s, GEICO began to stumble operationally due to suboptimal risk selection (or underwriting), under-reserving insurance claims,[7] and underperforming investments that cumulatively almost caused it to fail.[8] In response, the firm named Jack Byrne CEO in 1976, and he implemented a historic turnaround that returned GEICO to profitability;[9] however, after he left GEICO, it "embarked on some unwise diversification moves. This shift of emphasis away from its extraordinary core business stunted GEICO's growth, and by 1993, its market share had grown only fractionally, to 1.9 percent. Then Tony Nicely took charge [as CEO]."[10] Two years later, Warren Buffett took GEICO private.

Franchise Qualification

Warren Buffett followed GEICO for many years prior to taking it private; for example, he first wrote about the firm in 1951 when he was twenty-one years old. (The title of that article is "The Security I Like Best.")[11] His interest in GEICO never wavered, and it led to significant investments over time:

> Berkshire acquired GEICO in two stages. In 1976–80 we bought about one-third of the company's stock for $47 million.[12] Over the years, large repurchases by the company of its own shares

caused our position to grow to about 50 percent without our having bought any more shares. Then, on January 2, 1996, we acquired the remaining 50 percent of GEICO for $2.3 billion in cash, about 50 times the cost of our original purchase.[13]

Given his deep knowledge of the firm, Buffett was able to pick the best times to invest in GEICO. In practice, few acquirers have such an intimate knowledge of a target and therefore require screening approaches for opportunity identification/qualification purposes. One such approach is the Relative Profitability and Growth (RPG) matrix,[14] which is based on the three value drivers of profitability, growth, and the amount of time profitable growth can be sustained.[15] The RPG matrix is based on the simple idea that a firm outperforming its industry over time from both a profitability and growth perspective could be a franchise.[16]

As shown in **Figure 9.1**, the RPG matrix identifies a *franchise* (the upper–right quadrant) as a firm achieving greater levels of profitability and growth than its industry, which contrasts with

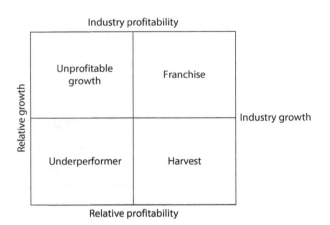

FIGURE 9.1 The Relative Profitability and Growth Matrix. *Source*: Joseph Calandro, Jr., and Scott Lane, "A New Competitive Analysis Tool: The Relative Profitability and Growth Matrix," *Strategy & Leadership* 35, no. 2 (2007): 31.

more profitable but slower growing firms, which are candidates for *harvesting* (or controlling reinvestment to maximize earnings; see the lower–right quadrant). The remaining categories follow similar logic. Despite the simplicity of this matrix, or perhaps because of it, it has proven useful in various industry analyses. Here it is used to qualify GEICO's franchise using return on equity (ROE) for profitability[17] and the change in net premium earned for growth.[18] Comparing GEICO to the insurance industry across these dimensions for the nine years prior to Buffett's acquisition gives the RPG profile presented in **Figure 9.2**.[19]

Note that only the right side of the matrix is displayed: the reason for this is that GEICO was more profitable than its industry over the entire assessment horizon, which is an obvious indication of a possible franchise. Note also how GEICO's relative performance breaks down into two distinct clusters:

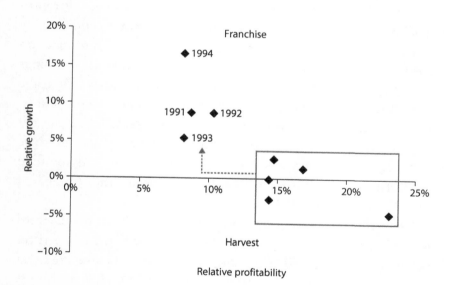

FIGURE 9.2 GEICO's Relative Profitability and Growth Matrix: 1986 to 1994. *Data sources*: GEICO 1994 Form 10K, Insurance Services Organization (ISO), and A. M. Best. Calculations are mine and have been rounded.

- 1986 to 1991, as represented by the five data points inside the rectangle within the figure, and
- 1991 to 1994, as represented by the remaining four data points.

Based on these clusters, it appears that GEICO changed strategic direction by trading off some relative profitability to achieve greater levels of relative growth (illustrated by the arrow in the exhibit) in order to firmly establish it as a franchise.[20] Validating this qualification is the objective of franchise valuation.

Franchise Valuation

By way of background, the modern version of value investing approaches valuation via a unique four-level continuum. The continuum begins with net asset value, which is derived by reproducing a balance sheet line by line so it is more economically consistent (in other words, it is based on estimated reproduction costs instead of booked historical costs). The next level is earnings power value, which is based on a level of past earnings that at the time of the valuation is expected to be sustainable into perpetuity. If the earnings power value is significantly greater than the net asset value, the firm could be a franchise, which is the only type of investment that creates value with growth, which is the final level of value. To illustrate, note the value profile that I prepared for GEICO in **Figure 9.3**.

Given this profile, the objective of franchise valuation—the third level of value along the continuum—is to identify the competitive advantage driving GEICO's $24.9 per share franchise premium shown in the exhibit *and* to determine if it is sustainable over time.

According to Michael Porter, "competitive advantage grows fundamentally out of value a firm is able to create for its buyers that exceeds the firm's cost of creating it,"[21] which is the

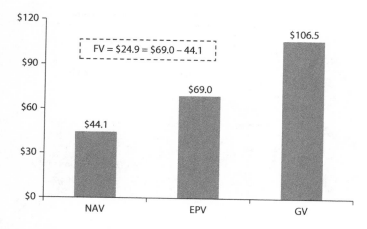

FIGURE 9.3 GEICO's Value Profile. *Source*: Joseph Calandro, Jr., *Applied Value Investing* (New York: McGraw-Hill, 2009), 56; see chapter 3 of that book for details. "NAV" is net asset value, "EPV" is earnings power value, "FV" is franchise value, and "GV" is growth value. All values are per share and are based solely on my valuation, which has been rounded. Compare this figure to the theoretical valuation model found in Bruce Greenwald, et al., *Value Investing— From Graham to Buffett & Beyond* (New York: Wiley, 2001), 44. A benefit of the modern value investing approach is that all investment assumptions are upfront in the valuation, not buried in a model or forecast. There is a process for deriving conservative, bottom-up valuation assumptions, which is profiled in the conclusion of my first book (Calandro [2009], 201–221). Briefly, professional value investors do *not* guess when making valuation assumptions; in fact, one thing that differentiates professional from amateur value investors is the rigor with which assumptions are approached and derived—in other words, the "information advantage" professional value investors bring to their work. This may—or should—sound obvious, but I continue to be surprised by how few nonprofessional value investors understand it, which is one of the reasons why I wrote the following paper and made it freely available for download: Joseph Calandro, Jr., *Value Investing General Principles* (September 21, 2016), available at SSRN: https://ssrn.com/abstract=2575429.

dynamic driving the franchise premium illustrated in **Figure 9.3**. There are two general forms of competitive advantage: having the lowest cost structure and competitive differentiation. These two advantages can be applied broadly across an entire industry or

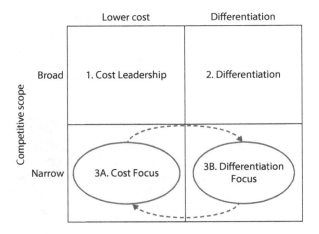

FIGURE 9.4 Basic Strategies and GEICO's Franchise. *Source:* Michael Porter, *Competitive Advantage* (New York: Free Press, 1998 [1985]), 12. I added the circles and dashed arrows.

narrowly to a targeted segment. Plotting these characteristics in a matrix illustrates the three basic competitive strategies shown in **Figure 9.4.**

As indicated above, GEICO was founded on a cost-focus strategy (the lower–left quadrant of **Figure 9.4**). Leo Godwin believed that if his firm pursued targeted customers directly, instead of through traditional insurance agent channels, it could lower its premium requirements that, coupled with relatively lower operating costs, would allow GEICO to outperform the competition in its market. To say this strategy was successfully implemented over time, and thereby generated economic returns, does not do it justice. Being the low-cost auto insurer allows GEICO to economically compete for the "safest" drivers, or drivers involved in fewer *and* less severe auto accidents on average over time. Thus, GEICO's relatively lower operating costs facilitate relatively lower loss costs over time, which is a dynamic that Warren Buffett and Tony Nicely have significantly leveraged, as will be shown below.

GEICO's returns did, however, turn to losses on two occasions due to poor reserving practices and poor diversification decisions. With regard to the latter, Porter observed that "Success can lead a focuser to lose sight of the reasons for its success and compromise its focus strategy for growth's sake."[22] In addition to lost focus, advantages can erode over time due to competition; for example, several researchers found that competitive advantages seem to generally have life spans of not more than ten years on average.[23] Applied to GEICO, these thoughts led to a significant strategic question facing Buffett in 1995. Is the management under Tony Nicely's leadership committed to both focusing on *and* sustaining GEICO's cost-focus-based competitive advantage over time (or a period of not less than ten years)? A positive answer to this question validates the franchise for valuation purposes, thereby allowing us to proceed to the fourth and final level of the continuum: growth.

Growth Valuation

Commenting on GEICO after he acquired it, Buffett noted that:

> [W]hen a company is selling a product with commodity-like economic characteristics, being the low-cost producer is all-important. This enduring competitive advantage of GEICO—one it possessed in 1951 when, as a 20-year-old student, I first became enamored with its stock—is the reason that over time it will inevitably increase its market share significantly while simultaneously achieving excellent profits.[24]

To quantify such an assessment, modern value investing theory approaches growth from two perspectives: normal growth and supernormal growth. Growth is considered "normal" if it results in a steady, upward-drifting cumulative growth curve with a slope greater than the firm's industry. Consider GEICO's cumulative growth curve for the years 1996 to 2018 in **Figure 9.5**.

Estimating the value of normal growth is accomplished by adjusting earnings power value by a growth multiple (see **Appendix 9.1** for the derivation). When applied to GEICO, it gives a growth value per share of $106.50, as shown in **Figure 9.3**.[25]

"Supernormal" growth, on the other hand, is defined by a period of dynamic growth that is followed by more normal levels. This approach is more applicable to venture capital deals; as such, it is only mentioned here for analytical completeness.

After valuing a target, negotiations to acquire it can begin. With respect to GEICO, Buffett initially attempted to take it private in a preferred share-to-stock swap deal valued at $55 per share (which had tax advantages over a cash deal). After a period of negotiation, GEICO asked for a price of $70 per share, cash or stock, which was rational per our valuation and given the involvement of Lou Simpson, who was GEICO's co-CEO and chief investment officer as well as a noted value investor in his own right. Buffett agreed to take the firm private at that price in a cash deal,[26] which based on our valuation means that he paid full earnings power value and therefore based this deal's margin of safety on its growth value.[27] The question at this point in the analysis becomes: how could GEICO realize this growth value?

Value Realization

In corporate M&A, once a deal closes, the valuation supporting it is seldom again consulted. In a growth–based franchise deal, however, valuations can be the starting point for value realization strategizing and planning. For example, in the GEICO case, our valuation established that the firm's franchise was built on a cost-focus strategy, which was successfully implemented pre-acquisition. GEICO's growth strategy at that time was based

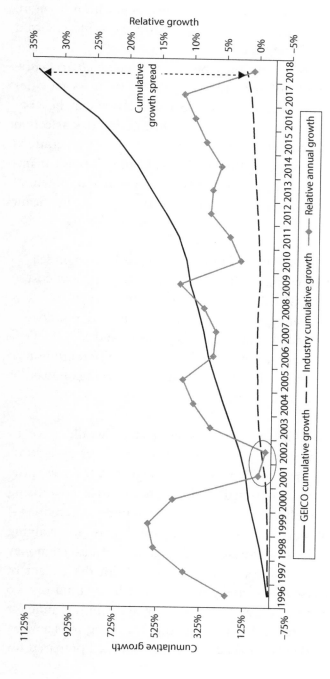

FIGURE 9.5 GEICO's Growth Profile: 1996 to 2018. *Data sources:* Berkshire Hathaway Shareholder Letters, Insurance Services Organization (ISO), and A. M. Best. Calculations are mine and have been rounded. The circle identifies the years in which GEICO grew less than its industry (along with the most recent year of 2018). GEICO's cumulative growth curve is a striking example of "normal growth," which is sometimes referred to as "controlled growth." See, for example, the GEICO discussion in Robert Hagstrom, *The Warren Buffett Way*, 3rd ed. (Hoboken, NJ: Wiley, 2004), 88.

predominantly on referrals; however, post-acquisition a more active growth strategy was required to realize the value reflected in the growth–based margin of safety.

Strategy formulation frequently begins with *value chain analysis*, which involves identifying and analyzing key business activities in linear fashion.[28] A basic insurance value chain can be constructed as follows: Marketing → Underwriting (or risk selection and pricing) → Ceded Reinsurance (or risk transfer) → Operations (or insurance processing) → Investment → Claims (or risk manifestation).[29] Every activity in a value chain is a source of potential differentiation, which is important because at GEICO a significant source of potential differentiation in 1995 was marketing:

- Underwriting, Operations, and Claims were focused on selling to and servicing "safe" drivers via efficient, low-cost operations per GEICO's core cost-focus strategy;
- Ceded Reinsurance was not a factor as Buffett did/does not hedge or cede his insurance exposures; and
- Investment is not a source of insurance differentiation (even though it is, obviously, a source of earnings power, as will be discussed below).

To be effective, GEICO's marketing strategy would have to differentiate the firm in a manner consistent with its core strategy as depicted by the circular arrows in **Figure 9.4**. As we now know, that strategy was based on highly innovative advertising campaigns that marketed one of the most mundane activities— buying personal automobile insurance—in highly entertaining ways around the firm's low-cost-based slogan: "I just saved money by switching my car insurance to GEICO." With the benefit of hindsight, we know this strategy worked, but how could one go about implementing and tracking a strategy like it in real time for value realization purposes? One useful tool for doing so is a *Management Matrix*. For example, consider the matrix I prepared for

GEICO in **Figure 9.6.** For simplicity, this matrix was structured on three basic forms of information: (1) the four popular *Balanced Scorecard* categories of Financial, Customer, Operational, and Learning & Growth,[30] (2) the two forms of competitive advantage (cost and differentiation), and (3) economies of scale.[31]

The measures profiled in the top portion of the Management Matrix give transparency to aspects of core franchise performance, and as such they should be identified and validated during the valuation and due diligence processes, as should the main drivers of the measures, which are listed in the bottom portion of the matrix. For example, each measure profiled in the exhibit was commented on by Warren Buffett either directly or indirectly in his shareholder letters from 1996 to 2009, which when aligned with the corresponding drivers clearly illuminate the dynamics of GEICO's franchise. Note that this framework is *not* meant to be a detailed performance scorecard or strategic analysis. It can, however, be used to summarize those analyses for managerial and value realization purposes as the following interpretation of **Figure 9.6** is meant to illustrate:

Financial: The customer-related cost drivers of GEICO's strategy are the amount of losses and related loss adjustment expenses generated by its customers (operating costs are addressed in the "Operational" and "Learning & Growth" sections below). As those customers are relatively "safer" than other drivers, they should, on average, file fewer *and* less severe loss claims, which should translate into pretax underwriting profit over time both absolute and relative to the insurance industry. By way of background, there are three core components of insurance company earnings: investment income and capital gains (losses), underwriting profit (loss), and the effects of ceded reinsurance.[32] As noted above, investment is not a source of insurance differentiation and Buffett does not use ceded reinsurance; hence, the strategic significance of underwriting profit to this insurance franchise. In addition, as shown in **Table 9.1,** GEICO's pretax underwriting profit vastly exceeded that of the insurance industry since it was taken private.

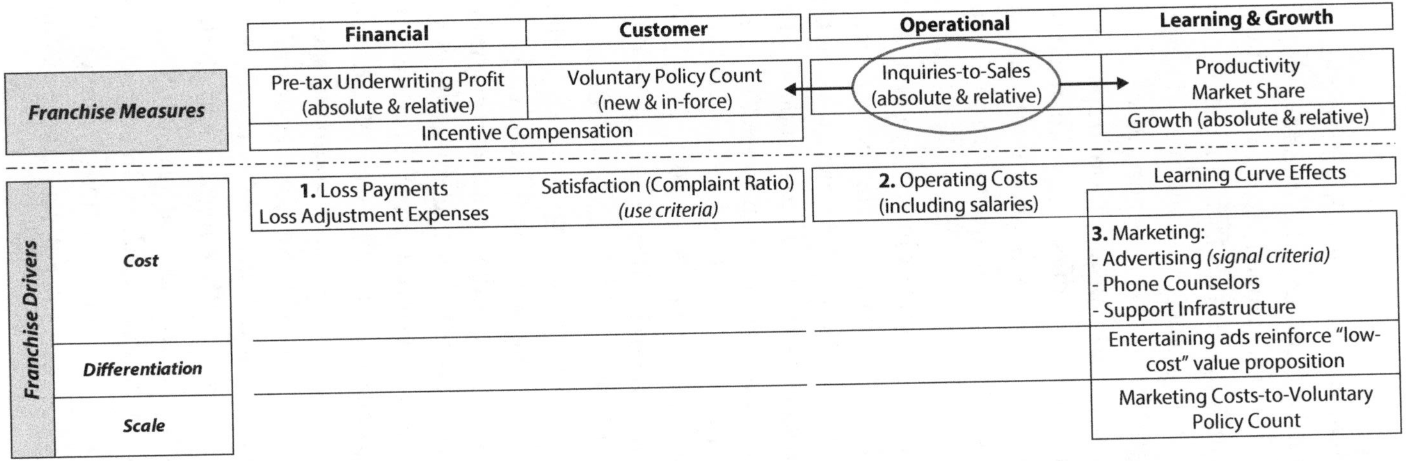

Financial	Customer	Operational	Learning & Growth
Pre-tax Underwriting Profit (absolute & relative)	Voluntary Policy Count (new & in-force)	Inquiries-to-Sales (absolute & relative)	Productivity Market Share Growth (absolute & relative)
Incentive Compensation			
1. Loss Payments Loss Adjustment Expenses	Satisfaction (Complaint Ratio) *(use criteria)*	**2.** Operating Costs (including salaries) Learning Curve Effects	**3.** Marketing: - Advertising *(signal criteria)* - Phone Counselors - Support Infrastructure
			Entertaining ads reinforce "low-cost" value proposition
			Marketing Costs-to-Voluntary Policy Count

Franchise Measures

Franchise Drivers: Cost, *Differentiation*, *Scale*

FIGURE 9.6 GEICO Management Matrix. *Note*: This Management Matrix is divided into two halves given the linkages of the categories: "Financial" and "Customer" strategic cost drivers are inherently linked, as are "Operational" and "Learning & Growth" drivers.

Table 9.1
Pre-tax Underwriting Profit: 1996 to 2018

| Year | Underwriting Income (in millions) | |
	GEICO Pretax	Industry Pretax
1996	$180	-$14,448
1997	$281	-$1,644
1998	$269	-$11,411
1999	$24	-$18,665
2000	-$224	-$26,480
2001	$221	-$49,751
2002	$416	-$27,767
2003	$452	-$3,062
2004	$970	$5,701
2005	$1,221	-$3,638
2006	$1,314	$31,115
2007	$1,113	$19,304
2008	$916	-$21,173
2009	$649	-$2,981
2010	$1,117	-$10,514
2011	$576	-$36,229
2012	$680	-$15,366
2013	$1,127	$15,247
2014	$1,159	$12,212
2015	$460	$8,949
2016	$462	-$4,708
2017	-$310	-$23,218
2018	$2,449	-$108
Total	**$13,072**	**-$178,646**

Data sources: Berkshire Hathaway Shareholder Letters, ISO, and A. M. Best. Calculations are the author's and have been rounded. Note: Even if an insurance company incurs a loss, it could still be profitable if the loss is less than market rates for money (Joseph Calandro and Scott Lane, "The Insurance Performance Measure: Bringing Value to the Insurance Industry," Journal of Applied Corporate Finance, 14, no. 4 [2002]: 94–99). For information on insurance company failures, see Best's Special Report: Impairment Review, a publication of A. M. Best.

Customer: GEICO's customer base is managed by first holding on to the relatively "safe" drivers that it already insures and then attracting others. The central measure of these activities is the number of voluntary policies it underwrites (non-voluntary policies being those that GEICO is forced to underwrite by regulators for the relatively unsafe drivers in "assigned risk pools"). A key driver of voluntary existing policies is the customers' level of satisfaction with GEICO's services; in other words, with GEICO's delivery on its promise to pay—as outlined in each insurance policy—after a claim is filed. If this is not done well it could result in regulatory and legal costs if complaints are filed, and it could also result in the loss of future business. Therefore, Buffett carefully tracked/tracks GEICO's complaint ratio,[33] which as a measure reflects what strategists refer to as "use value."[34]

Significantly, GEICO's incentive compensation is based on the above two metrics (underwriting profit and the number of voluntary policies underwritten), as Buffett explained:

> The bonuses received by dozens of top executives, starting with [CEO] Tony [Nicely], are based upon only two key variables: (1) growth in voluntary auto policies and (2) underwriting profitability on "seasoned" auto business (meaning policies that have been on the books for more than one year). In addition, we use the same yardsticks to calculate the annual contribution to the company's profit-sharing plan. *Everyone at GEICO knows what counts* (italics added).[35]

Aligning incentives to clear objectives is fundamental to efficient value realization over time, as is ensuring that a firm's objective, the strategy underlying it, measures tracking it, and incentives aligned to it generally do not change over time. Buffett is clearly aware of this; for example, he observed that "at Berkshire, we never greet good work by raising the bar. If GEICO's performance continues to improve, we will happily keep on making larger [performance] charts."[36] This management approach, while logical and consistent with long-term value realization, is not always employed in this age of stretch-goal management.

Operational: An operational measure at GEICO that heavily influences value realization is the number of insurance inquiries compared to the number of insurance policies sold (absolute and relative to prior years). The dual influence, and thus importance, of this measure to GEICO's franchise is illustrated in **Figure 9.6** by arrows pointing toward the "Customer" and "Learning & Growth" categories. This influence is cost sensitive because the human resources and marketing activities upon which it is based can be expensive. However, these costs can be mitigated, as will be shown immediately below, which is strategically significant because, as noted above, the firm's relatively lower cost structure is the foundation of its competitive advantage *and* the driver of its sustainability.

Learning & Growth: The benefits of increased productivity are straightforward: "The company producing more with a given set of inputs (capital, labor, and materials) or using fewer inputs to produce the same output has an advantage over the company producing less."[37] In other words, operating costs will decline if employees become more efficient over time. The *learning curve* formalizes this concept and "is based on the statistical finding that as the cumulative output doubles, the cumulative average labor input time required per unit will be reduced by some constant percentage, ranging between 10 percent and 40 percent."[38] While I do not know the specific learning strategies GEICO employed, it is undeniable that the firm realized learning curve effects over time as the following quote illustrates: "between year-end 2003 and year-end 2006, the number of GEICO policies increased from 5.7 million to 8.1 million, a jump of 42 percent. Yet during that same period, the company's employees (measured on a full-time-equivalent basis) fell 3.5 percent. So productivity grew 47 percent. And GEICO didn't start fat."[39] Productivity continued to improve through 2008 as Buffett reported:

No one likes to buy auto insurance. But virtually everyone likes to drive. So, sensibly, drivers look for the lowest-cost insurance consistent with first-class service. Efficiency is the key to low cost, and efficiency is Tony [Nicely]'s specialty. Five years ago the number of policies per employee was 299. In 2008, the number was 439, a huge increase in productivity.[40]

Turning to growth, GEICO's cumulative growth and relative growth curves are shown in **Figure 9.5**. Another strategic growth measure is market share, which Buffett comments on regularly when reporting on GEICO's results, and with good reason: in 1995, when he took GEICO private, its market share was 2.5 percent; by 2012, it was 9.7 percent, which means GEICO's share grew by a compounded annual rate of 7.8 percent.[41] A strategic driver of that growth was the more effective signaling of GEICO's value proposition through advertising, which powerfully differentiated the firm from its competition.

GEICO's highly impressive growth was obviously not without cost; in 2007, Buffett reported that from 1995 to 2006 GEICO's advertising budget grew from $31 million to $751 million.[42] However, advertising costs are subject to *economies of scale* (unit costs decline as unit sales increase), which is strategically significant in this case.

In closing this section, it is important to note that the activities underlying a Management Matrix (in the case of GEICO, low-cost insurance products and innovative advertising) interact continuously and therefore must be managed systemically, efficiently, and consistently over time. Effective management is also important for competitive reasons because the profit and growth generated by a franchise will increasingly attract the attention of competitors.

Competition and Conclusion

In 1995, GEICO was the sixth-largest personal automobile insurer in the United States; by 2009, it was the third largest[43] (after State

Farm and Allstate). By mid-2018, GEICO was the second-largest, after State Farm. Not surprisingly, both State Farm and Allstate have tried to copy GEICO's marketing strategy to some extent. Nevertheless, when considering GEICO's competition, Progressive Insurance is the firm that frequently comes to mind because it operates under a similar cost-focus strategy. **Figure 9.7** illustrates both firms' cumulative growth curves.

During the assessment horizon both of these insurers cumulative growth curves are currently at the same general level. GEICO's growth curve, however, is much smoother, which was accomplished profitability except for the years 2000 and 2017 (**Table 9.1**). Therefore, the GEICO franchise still appears sustainable twenty-five years after its acquisition. This value judgment is the logical outcome of an innovative strategy, which was successfully executed by focused and disciplined management to realize value over time.

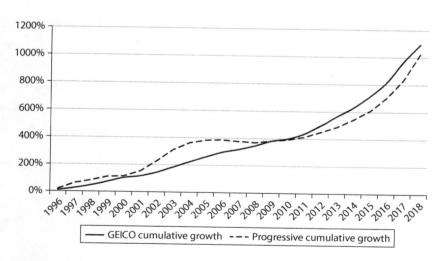

FIGURE 9.7 GEICO and Progressive Cumulative Growth Curves: 1996 to 2018. *Data sources*: Berkshire Hathaway and Progressive annual reports. Calculations are mine and have been rounded.

By their very nature, franchises like GEICO are scarce and difficult to find. However, if one is found—possibly with an RPG matrix (**Figure 9.2**)—and if it can be taken private at a reasonable margin of safety, it will offer a lucrative investment opportunity (**Figure 9.3**). Realizing the value of such opportunities has proven difficult in the past; however, frameworks such as a Management Matrix (**Figure 9.6**) can help shed light on the strategically significant components of a franchise. Under the stewardship of effective corporate managers, growth–based franchises can realize significant value over time just as Warren Buffett and Tony Nicely have at GEICO (**Figure 9.5** and **Table 9.1**).

APPENDIX 9.1

Note on Estimating Growth Value

"A simple mathematical connection can be established between calculated *normal current* earnings and expected average *future* earnings, based on the rate of growth assumed."
—BENJAMIN GRAHAM, DAVID DODD, AND
SIDNEY COTTLE (ITALICS ORIGINAL)[1]

"Growth can add to the value when the return on invested capital is above average, thereby assuming that when a dollar is being invested in the company, at least one dollar of market value is being created. However, growth for a business earning low returns on capital can be detrimental to shareholders."
—ROBERT HAGSTROM[2]

THIS APPENDIX is somewhat technical and was requested by several academicians interested in value investing–based growth valuation. It is therefore provided for completeness and is not necessary for the implementation of the approach profiled in the chapter.

As noted in the chapter, there are two forms of growth: the normal, steady growth of a sustainable franchise and supernormal growth. Considering normal growth first, modern value investing theory established the equivalence of net asset value and earnings power value for firms that are not franchises—firms not operating with sustainable competitive advantages *and* not suffering from performance issues, which can be denoted as follows:

$$V = (NAV \approx EPV) \qquad (1)$$

where

  V is value
  NAV is net asset value
  EPV is earnings power value

Traditionally, value is estimated via the present value of discounted earnings (or cash flows) as follows:

$$V = \sum_{n=1}^{\infty} E_n / (1 + K)^n \tag{2}$$

where

  E is earnings
  K is the required rate of return

If the level of earnings is sustainable at a constant level forever, which is a fundamental EPV assumption, then equation (2) reduces to:

$$V = E / K \tag{3}$$

Constant, sustainable earnings are a function of net asset value and the return on that value, and as such, equation (3) can be restated as:

$$V = (NAV * RNAV) / K \tag{4}$$

where

  $RNAV$ is the return on net asset value = E / NAV

Dividing by net asset value gives:

$$V / NAV = RNAV / K \tag{5}$$

Equation (1) holds when the right side of equation (5) relatively equals one; when that ratio materially exceeds one, however, the equation becomes:

$$V = (NAV + FV) = EPV \tag{6}$$

where

FV is franchise value

Equation (6) is illustrated in **Figure 9.3**. Substituting in equation (5) and then solving for the value of a growing franchise gives:

$$GV = (RNAV/K) * EPV \qquad (7)$$

where

GV is growth value of a sustainable franchise

This derivation draws on Benjamin Esty, *Note on Value Drivers*, HBS Case Services #9-297-082, April 7, 1997, and William E. Fruhan, Jr., *Financial Strategy: Studies in the Creation, Transfer, and Destruction of Shareholder Value* (Homewood, IL: Irwin, 1979). It is also consistent with the multiplier approach of Benjamin Graham, David Dodd, and Sidney Cottle, *Security Analysis*, 4th ed. (New York: McGraw-Hill, 1962 [1934]), 507. Further, it relates growth to current values, which those authors felt—correctly in my view—was so important (vi).

Supernormal growth, in comparison, is composed of two parts or phases. During phase 1, the growth experienced is dynamic (in other words, nonlinear), which over time transitions to a more normal, steady level that characterizes phase 2 growth. Phase 1 growth can be estimated by present value analysis, which Professor Greenwald and his coauthors denote as follows:[3]

$$PV = (RNAV - g)/(K - g) * EPV \qquad (8)$$

where

PV = the present value of abnormal growth

g = expected growth rate

Because supernormal growth is a function of both dynamic growth *and* the normal growth of a franchise, it is a function of equations (8) and (7). Employing substitution "and a little alge-braic manipulation" gives the below equation:[4]

$$M = 1 - (g/K) \, (K/RNAV)/1 - (g/K) \qquad (9)$$

where

M = supernormal growth multiple

As explained above, the multiple used to estimate the steady growth of a sustainable franchise is simply $RNAV/K$, which when multiplied by EPV gives the GV (equation (7)).

The procedure for estimating supernormal growth is a little more involved: first, the amount of growth for each year of phase 1 must be estimated (typical durations are five to ten years). Phase 2 growth estimation follows by way of a terminal value. These esti-mates must then be discounted to the present. Once a present value is obtained, it is multiplied by M (equation (9)) to get the supernormal growth value.[5]

To help analyze the relationship of normal growth and super-normal growth multiples, Professor Greenwald and his coauthors presented the matrix shown in **Table 9.A.1**.

Table 9.A.1
Modern Graham and Dodd Growth Value Multiple Matrix

	(A)	(B)	(C)	(D)	(E)
RNAV/K	1.0	1.5	2.0	2.5	3.0
(1) g/K 0.25	1.00	1.11	1.17	1.20	1.22
(2) g/K 0.50	1.00	1.33	1.50	1.60	1.67
(3) g/K 0.75	1.00	2.00	2.50	2.80	3.00

Source: Bruce Greenwald, et al., *Value Investing: From Graham to Buffett and Beyond* (New York: Wiley, 2001), 144 except that Return on Net Asset Value (*RNAV*) replaces Return on Capital (ROC) and the notation *K* is used for the discount rate instead of *R*.

The shaded row in the exhibit reflects the multiple calculated in equation (7) while the main body of the matrix contains the M multiple of equation (9). As can be seen, it takes a great deal to triple either growth multiple, normal or supernormal, and therefore investors and corporate managers alike must proceed with growth–based investments cautiously and conservatively. Indeed, one lesson of financial history is that even the most skilled investors incur losses when they fail to do this. Consider, for example, J. P. Morgan's experience with International Mercantile Marine (IMM) in the early 1900s, which owned RMS *Titanic*,[6] and Warren Buffett's experience with General Re in the late 1990s to early 2000s.[7] Clearly, if these two financial titans can misjudge the value of growth, the rest of us are at risk of doing so.

10

Value Realization at GTI Corporation

"If price changes for the most part will reflect current developments rather than the future . . . then good judgment as to what is in store should prove unusually profitable. In other words, there should be excellent opportunities to act ahead of the market. The man who is sure improvement is coming can buy on the basis of current less favorable conditions, and thus derive the full benefit of the betterment—if it materializes."
—BENJAMIN GRAHAM[1]

"Second-level thinkers know that, to achieve superior results, they have to have an edge in either information or analysis, or both."
—HOWARD MARKS[2]

A KEY THEME of this book is the importance of some kind of information and/or analytical advantage, which is something a corporate manager knows that other corporate managers either do not know or choose to ignore. While this may sound simple, I assure you that it is anything but. Having an "advantage" inherently means doing something different,[3] and the population of corporate and investment managers who are truly different is exceedingly small.[4]

A reason the majority of corporate and investment managers act alike is that there is safety in numbers. Nevertheless, sometimes circumstances force differentiation, which is what happened in the case that is the subject of this chapter. A firm experienced significant performance issues, and as a result its new executive manager employed a financial distress model to inform his managerial activities, which helped realize significant value.

By way of background, thousands of articles, papers, and books have been written on the subject of "analytics," and yet almost none of this literature pertains to how analytical output should be used. Therefore, it should come as no surprise that so many people either misuse or abuse such output.[5] Consider Roger Lowenstein's book *When Genius Failed*, which profiled the failure of the hedge fund Long-Term Capital Management (LTCM). This fund was managed by several leading bond traders at the time, as well as a number of finance professors, two of whom won the Nobel Prize in Economics. Despite this pedigree, LTCM infamously failed. According to Lowenstein:

> The professors' conceit was to think that models could forecast the limits of behavior. In fact, the models could tell them what was reasonable or what was predictable based on the past. The professors overlooked the fact that people, traders included, are not always reasonable. This is the true lesson of Long-Term's demise. No matter what the models say, traders are not machines guided by silicon chips; they are impressionable and imitative; they run in flocks and retreat in hordes.[6]

This example is not meant to imply that modeled output is useless; in fact, some models are extremely useful when used properly. For example, Professors Robert Carton and Charles Hofer tested a variety of performance measures and related models and found that the change in the Altman bankruptcy prediction model (popularly known as the Z-score model) tested the highest.[7,8] I profile this model below before explaining how it was successfully used in the historic GTI Corporation turnaround.

The Z-score Model

Professor Emeritus Edward I. Altman introduced the Z-score model in 1968.[9] He used a statistical technique called discriminate analysis to create his financial distress prediction model, which has generated insightful results ever since.[10]

In constructing his model, Altman used basic financial ratios as inputs thereby making the resulting model inherently practical, in contrast to so many other financial models. The general form of the Z-score model for publicly held firms is shown below:

$$Z = 1.2X_1 + 1.4X_2 + 3.3X_3 + 0.6X_4 + 1.0X_5 \qquad (1)$$

where
  Z = Z-score
  X_1 = working capital / total assets
  X_2 = retained earnings / total assets
  X_3 = earnings before interest and taxes / total assets
  X_4 = market value of equity / book value of total liabilities
  X_5 = sales / total assets

The criteria used to interpret Z-scores are

- **Safe Zone** = $Z > 2.99$; the firm is not at risk of financial distress,
- **Distress Zone** = $Z < 1.81$; the firm will likely go bankrupt, and
- **Gray Zone** = $1.81 \leq Z \leq 2.99$; the firm is at risk of financial distress.

The Z-score can be modified for privately held firms as shown below:

$$Z = 6.56X_1 + 3.26X_2 + 6.72X_3 + 1.05X_4 \qquad (2)$$

where
  X_1 = working capital / total assets
  X_2 = retained earnings / total assets

X_3 = earnings before interest and taxes / total assets
X_4 = net worth / total liabilities

The criteria used to interpret this model are

- **Safe Zone** = $Z > 2.60$,
- **Distress Zone** = $Z < 1.10$, and
- **Gray Zone** = $1.10 \leq Z \leq 2.60$.

The Z-score has been influential in areas such as credit risk analysis, distressed investing,[11] M&A target analysis, and commercial insurance underwriting. It has not, however, generally been associated with performance management or value realization activities irrespective of the fact that, per equation (1) above, the market value of equity is incorporated into the model as the numerator of the X_4 factor. In addition, performance management scholars Robert S. Kaplan and David P. Norton listed "survival" as the first financial goal profiled in their seminal paper on the *Balanced Scorecard*,[12] which the Z-score measures. More importantly for our purposes, the Z-score is a measure of creditworthiness, which the late value investor Marty Whitman found more strategically useful than the market value of equity because, among other things, it affords management options to be opportunistic with their superior financial position when others may be forced to either sell or pull back strategically given distressed conditions.

The Z-score model has insightfully measured creditworthiness since it was introduced. Nevertheless, Professors Carton and Hofer are two of the very few to make this connection in a performance management context,[13] and the first—as far as I am aware—to have statistically tested it. Given the strength of these authors' findings, I researched the use of the Z-score in a corporate management context and uncovered the following case study, which provides insight into how analytical models in general can be used by corporate managers to realize value.

GTI Corporation

During the 1960s, the GTI Corporation (GTI) was an electronic components manufacturing firm.[14] Early in the decade, GTI embarked on a powerful growth strategy that was significantly financed with debt, which was a relatively common strategy at the time (much like it is today). However, as the U.S. economy slowed between 1969 and 1972, leveraged firms such as GTI experienced difficulty servicing their debt (leveraged firms of today, circa mid-2018, take note).

In May 1975, GTI's financial difficulties passed a relatively critical threshold: erroneous information was inadvertently reported to the American Stock Exchange, which listed the firm's stock. This discovery prompted GTI's president to resign and served as the catalyst for the appointment of board member James K. La Fleur as the new chairman and CEO, which came with a mandate to resolve GTI's difficulties, turn around its performance, and realize the value of the firm's equity.

Prior to his appointment, La Fleur served as the CEO of his own firm where he served on the audit committee of its board of directors. Given this background, he was well positioned to manage GTI "by the numbers," which is to say by the fundamentals. This type of approach can, at times, be enabled by analytical models to both evaluate the financial impact of potential initiatives and track performance over time. During his review of GTI's performance, La Fleur recalled an article on the Z-score model, which he decided to use in his managerial efforts. Inserting GTI's financial data from 1972 to 1975 into the Z-score model results in the profile illustrated in **Figure 10.1**.

As can be seen, from 1974 to 1975, GTI's Z-score plunged into the *Distress Zone* from the *Safe Zone*. This was extremely troubling to La Fleur when he learned that the Z-score had up to a 95 percent accuracy rate predicting bankruptcy when "based on data from approximately one year prior to failure."[15] Interestingly,

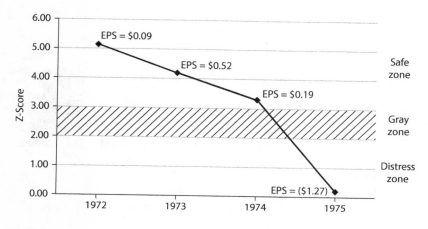

FIGURE 10.1 GTI Corporation Z-score: 1972 to 1975. *Source*: Edward I. Altman.

and as also illustrated in the exhibit, even though GTI's Z-score declined from 1972 to 1973, its earnings per share (EPS) during that same period of time increased rather dramatically from $0.09 to $0.52. In 1974, however, both GTI's Z-score and its EPS declined, but at $0.19, its EPS was still much higher than it had been in 1972. This value suggests that, over time, the change in Z-score better reflected GTI's financial condition than the change in its EPS did. Carton and Hofer did not include EPS growth in their study, but they did include both operating cash flow and the change in cash flow over time and neither tested as significantly as the change in Z-score did.[16]

Identifying the drivers of Z-score change, positive and negative, can be accomplished through an understanding of how Z-score factors change over time. Consider the profile of GTI's Z-score factors from 1972 to 1975 that is illustrated in **Figure 10.2**. This profile illustrates the performance-related insights that can be gained from a study of the Z-score over time. However, La Fleur decided to take Z-score analysis a step further; specifically, he planned to use the model as a screening device with which

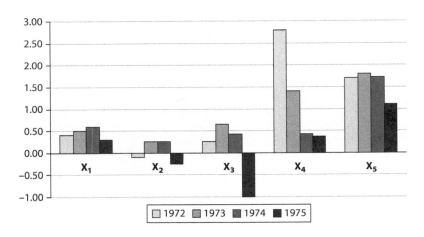

FIGURE 10.2 GTI Corporation Z-score Ratio Analysis: 1972 to 1975. *Source*: Edward I. Altman.

to "work backwards" to strategic initiatives that would improve GTI's performance as measured by the Z-score.[17]

La Fleur planned to use the Z-score as both a strategic assessment and a performance management tool to realize value at GTI. To demonstrate how he accomplished this, consider the composition of the X_1 factor in equation (1) above, which is the ratio of working capital / total assets. While analyzing GTI's working capital, La Fleur discovered that its inventory management processes were suboptimal; therefore, initiatives were designed to improve those processes with the results being tracked by the Z-score.

Additionally, in an effort to increase operating earnings and thereby increase the numerator of the X_3 factor in equation (1), La Fleur trimmed staff and then solicited the input of GTI's employees to formulate initiatives designed to resolve some of the firm's performance issues. Involving employees in the initiative formulation process ensured early buy-in and increased the probability of successful execution, which was a very wise managerial decision.

Initiatives such as those mentioned above improved GTI's performance as measured by incremental Z-score improvement; however, given the extent of GTI's difficulties, and the extent to which those difficulties were generated from flawed growth and funding strategies, divestiture was clearly an option that La Fleur had to consider. In addition, as four of the Z-score's five factors in equation (1) have total assets in the denominator, divesting uneconomic assets would materially and substantially drive Z-score improvement. Toward that end, and subsequent to further analyses, La Fleur concluded that GTI's Crystal Base business unit was both capital intensive and at risk of coming under competitive pressure, which is a potent combination; therefore, it was identified as a candidate for divestment. Additionally, Crystal Base's quartz crystal product line was not core to GTI's electronic components business. Therefore, in late 1976, GTI sold Crystal Base for $1,348,000 in cash and notes, the cash being used to pay down debt.[18]

The results of La Fleur's various Z-score-informed initiatives were impressive. As illustrated in **Figure 10.3**, GTI's Z-score increased dramatically from a low of 0.38 in 1975, which was

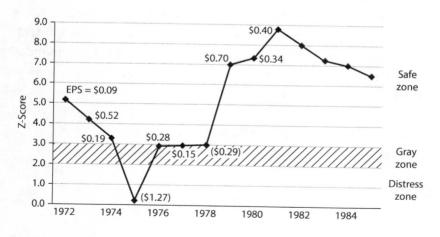

FIGURE 10.3 GTI Corporation Z-score: 1972 to 1984. *Source*: Edward I. Altman.

clearly in the *Distress Zone*, to 2.95, which was on the border of the *Gray* and *Safe Zones* in 1976.[19] GTI's Z-score held at this relative level for two years, until 1979, when it increased an incredible four points to approximately 7.0, which was well within the *Safe Zone*. This significant increase, which is also illustrated in **Figure 10.3**, was caused by another divestiture that was also informed by Z-score-based analysis.

The value realized by La Fleur's initiatives was as impressive as the firm's Z-score recovery was. The market value of GTI's equity increased 57 percent on a compounded basis from the (presumably) 1975 low of $1,000,000 to the $15,000,000 high set in 1980.[20] Such results reconcile with the findings of Carton and Hofer that the change in Z-score provides substantial relative information about performance management and resulting value realization.

Conclusion

James La Fleur demonstrated significant skill in *operations* by trimming staff and then soliciting the input of employees to formulate initiatives designed to resolve some of GTI's performance issues. He also demonstrated *investment* skill by divesting noncore GTI assets, the proceeds of which were used to pay down debt. Knowing when to pay down debt is a very important *financial* consideration that is frequently overlooked until some form of distress occurs. These three capabilities of modern security analysis and corporate management were identified by the late Marty Whitman (see **Chapter 7**). The next chapter presents another case study on this theme, but on a much larger scale.

11

Value Realization at the Union Pacific

"We have no right to reject the lessons of the past until we have at least studied and understood them."
—BENJAMIN GRAHAM[1]

"Between 1879 and 1881 [Jay] Gould erected a business empire of such magnitude and with such breathtaking swiftness that the railroad industry would never be the same again. Of all business titans of his age, none managed to accomplish so much with so little so quickly. The extraordinary chain of events that would elevate Gould into a legendary figure began with his attempt to restore the fortunes of the Union Pacific."
—MAURY KLEIN[2]

"REJECTING THE LESSONS of the past" has occurred generation after generation and will no doubt continue to occur in the future, human nature being what it is. Once a dominant narrative becomes established, it is very difficult to change it, even when the facts are incontrovertible. This has certainly been the case with the corporate manager profiled in this chapter, the late Jay Gould. No one in U.S. financial and business history is as misunderstood, and underappreciated, as Jay Gould.[3] There are a number of reasons why.

First, Gould was an intensely private man who did not engage with the press unless he wanted something specific from them. In other words, he used the press to achieve his desired ends, not to advance theirs. Second, Gould was uncommonly successful in investment, speculation/trading, and corporate management due to a variety of strategic moves that were frequently so fast, audacious, and complex that few people understood what he was doing or why. Third, Gould did not socialize with the "elite," preferring instead to spend his free time with his family and his books.[4] Over time, all of these factors coalesced into an information vacuum, and as social systems, like nature in general, abhor a vacuum, information was generated to fill it whether it was factually accurate or not.

Regarding "the facts" about Gould, I am doing something different in this chapter. I am going to begin at the end of the story to illustrate the value he realized at the Union Pacific Railroad (UP) during his managerial tenure there before profiling how he did it.

The compounded annual growth rate of the UP's stock price from December 24, 1874, to December 24, 1880, when Gould managed the firm, is 19 percent, which is impressive in and of itself but all the more so compared to the 7.5 percent compounded annual growth rate (price-weighted) of the New York Stock Exchange over the same general time period.[5] It is important to note two things while considering this performance: the U.S. economy was both in a major depression *and* generally deflationary from October 1873—following the infamous financial panic—to March 1879,[6] and there was no monetary stimulus like quantitative easing (QE) so Gould was operating against significant monetary headwinds,[7] which makes his achievement all the more impressive.

This chapter is structured in three sections: the first broadly profiles the celebrated life of Jay Gould, the second presents a framework that puts his various activities into analytical context, and the final section outlines practical recommendations that may be of interest to modern corporate managers.

Profile of Jay Gould[8]

Born in 1836 on a farm near Roxbury, New York, Jay Gould had a passion for education. Shortly before his sixteenth birthday, he left home to work for a surveyor. He taught himself surveying

and wrote an impressive history of Delaware County. Gould subsequently won the trust of a prominent tanner and at twenty set
out to build and run a tannery from scratch. Despite his youth,
older workers respected him well enough that the settlement was
named Gouldsboro.

Tanning occupied him until 1860, when an unfortunate part-
nership with the Charles M. Leupp firm unraveled. Gould then
turned his attention to Wall Street. Despite being a financial out-
sider, he not only survived but also gradually mastered the intricacies of "no holds barred" finance. Unlike many investors on Wall
Street, his approach was quiet, subtle, and self-deprecating. He
learned well the art of being underestimated and acting contrary
to "conventional wisdom" as it existed on nineteenth-century
Wall Street.

For seven years, Gould gradually improved his fortunes. He
was secretive, telling no one about an operation except those
directly involved, and even then only as much as he wanted them
to know. He added a view of ethical and legal niceties that, at
times, bordered on amorality, *but* that was common in his day.
Gould entered Wall Street on the eve of the Civil War, a time when
the rules became, shall we say, malleable amid the opportunities
afforded by wartime.[9]

Two legendary episodes catapulted him from obscurity to notoriety. In 1867 and 1868, Gould joined forces with Daniel Drew
and Jim Fisk to outmaneuver Cornelius Vanderbilt in the "Erie
War" that ended with Gould and Fisk in control of the Erie
Railroad. And in 1869, he conceived of a scheme to corner the
nation's gold supply that culminated in the "Black Friday" panic.
Together, these episodes both enhanced and blackened Gould's
reputation, resulting in a steady stream of abuse from the press
that helped shape his reputation as the most hated man on Wall
Street, which continues to this day.

Frankly, that reputation is undeserved. Unlike many "titans"
of his age, Gould lived a quiet, extremely private life unmarred

by personal excess. He shunned high society, was devoted to his wife and six children, created an extensive personal library of books that he actually read, and built the largest privately owned greenhouse in the nation. Contrary to the image of him as a lone wolf, he formed close associations with colleagues that lasted his lifetime. For example, Collis Huntington, one of Gould's most bitter rivals,[10] praised Gould's reliability: "I know there are many people who do not like him . . . I will say that I always found that he would do just as he agreed to do."[11]

Having succeeded as a financial speculator/trader, Gould turned his sights to business. Specifically, he applied his financial expertise to the problems of railroad management at the Erie by devising a bold strategy that forced Vanderbilt to revise his handling of the New York Central Railroad and begin expanding westward to Chicago and beyond.[12]

After being ousted from the Erie in 1872, Gould pursued his career on Wall Street while awaiting a suitable opportunity to take hold of another railroad. It came at the end of 1873 when Gould bought heavily into the UP. Part of the first transcontinental road completed in May 1869, the Union Pacific–Central Pacific remained the only rail line from the Missouri River to the Pacific Coast. Like the Erie, it was a big, oversold property that was in distress following the Credit Mobilier scandal of 1873 and a history of inept management.

In winning the trust of the UP's major stockholders, Gould promised that he would restore the railroad's financial credibility, improve its operations, formulate its strategy, and boost its stock price. Within a year, he turned around its financial position by clearing up the floating debt and refunding its income bonds. Operationally, he turned the company around through close attention to the details of every aspect of its operation.

Jay Gould stayed with the UP for six years, leaving only when it became clear that he could not solve the "financial albatross" of the government debt. Contrary to popular belief, the government bonds issued to help construct the UP were not a subsidy but a loan.[13] Further, the UP was one of very few railroads with a federal rather than state charter, which made it directly beholden to Congress. The task of reaching a settlement on the debt with various members of Congress proved too much for Gould so he sold his UP stock to monetize his share of the value illustrated in **Figure 11.1**.

Gould used the proceeds to put together a new southwestern rail system built around the Missouri Pacific Railroad, which ran from St. Louis to Kansas City. This new system played a major role in the economic development of the Southwest, which Gould continued to manage until his death in 1892.

Investor, Financier, and Operator

To realize value like Jay Gould did at the UP—and in a troubled economy without government assistance, no less—requires a broad set of integrated skills. Prior to controlling the UP, Gould had been both a successful speculator/trader and investor. As a speculator, he concentrated on shorter-term market movements while as an investor he focused on longer-term values. Each of these activities require a different skill set; as such, it is rare to find someone who is successful at both investing and speculating, even in our own time. For example, Warren Buffett is a well-known investor who profits from the successful strategic execution of the firms he owns over time while George Soros is a well-known speculator/trader who moves in and out of trades to profit from market trends or trend changes. These classifications are general in nature as Buffett has traded in the past and Soros has invested, but the point of the example is clear: longer-term investors and shorter-term speculators/traders are known for their different skill sets. Because Gould operated as both an investor and speculator/trader, he is difficult to classify at even the highest level like we did with Buffett and

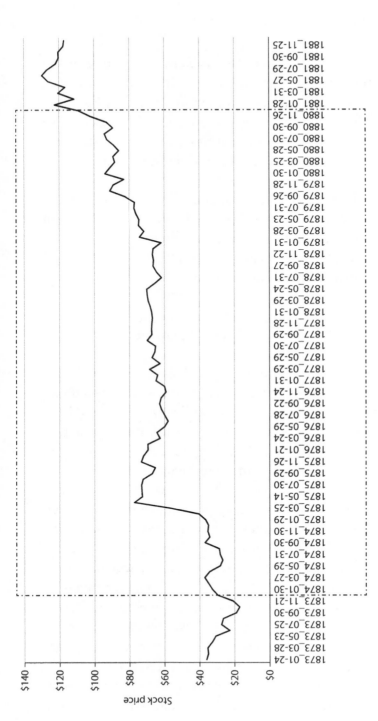

FIGURE 11.1 Select Union Pacific (UP) stock prices from 1873 to 1881. *Notes:* The data source is the *Commercial and Financial Chronicle*, https://catalog.hathitrust.org/Record/000548353, for the years 1873 to 1881. Thanks to Kristin Aguilera and Bob Wright of the Museum of American Finance in New York for referring me to this source. The dotted rectangle encloses the years that Jay Gould controlled the UP (1874 to 1880). As noted in the chapter, "control" means setting the direction of the firm rather than owning a majority interest in it. Gould exercised control by dominating the UP governance structure as a major, albeit not majority, shareholder. The figure displays one stock price for each month of the years profiled (every other month is labeled on the x-axis). No one consistent date each month is used so the chart should only be considered representative of UP performance over the profiled timeframe.

Soros. For example, Gould's gold speculation earned him a fair bit of notoriety, but his investment in the Erie Railroad, from both the buy and sell sides, was timed perfectly, which enabled him to invest in the UP at margin of safety–based prices.[14]

Gould also exhibited a level of financial expertise that rivaled the top bankers of his day, including the legendary J. P. Morgan. For example, the UP was debt heavy when he assumed control of it, but he effectively restructured it within a year.[15] He accomplished this through a combination of aggressive negotiating, innovative financing (which included Gould assuming some of the debt himself), and leveraging the relationships across his wide financial network.[16] This is an important detail because financing expertise enabled him to economically fund his activities at the UP in a way that is highly relevant today. For example, consider the results of the 2005 acquisition of Hertz Global Holdings, which have been summarized by the late Marty Whitman as follows: "Clearly, the principal contributing factor to the success of the sponsors [i.e., Clayton Dubilier and Rice, the Carlyle Group, and the Merrill Lynch Private Equity Fund] and their investors has been the sponsors' enormous ability and enormous credibility in accessing capital markets on a super-attractive basis."[17]

Finally, Gould was an extremely effective railroad operator,[18] something that virtually all of his detractors have ignored. The official history of the UP notes that "everyone knew of [his] genius for finance but no one suspected his capacity for mastering every phase of railroad building. His alert eye caught every detail, grasped every possibility. He did his homework with a thoroughness that astounded less driven men."[19] This drive enabled him to discover new sources of revenue for the UP,[20] devise ways to better use the road's land, and keep a "close monitoring of costs."[21] The results profiled in **Figure 11.1** vividly support this assessment.

In sum, Jay Gould simultaneously deployed a broad array of capabilities—operational, investment, and financial—to realize value at the UP. Prior to making a move, however, Gould formulated a strategic view that he wanted to execute. Adding strategy to the managerial capability mix results in the framework illustrated in **Figure 11.2**.

Strategy: There are many ways to approach corporate strategy; I use here a "finite opportunity" approach rather than the more traditional "sustainable competitive advantage" approach. The reason is that Jay Gould seemed hardwired to be flexible when it came to strategy, switching gears quickly when a strategy did not prove itself and/or a better one presented itself. This flexibility is consistent with his speculating/trading background and, interestingly, it is consistent with modern "complexity economics," which holds that *no* strategy is sustainable. Such a position necessarily "changes our definition of an excellent company from one that

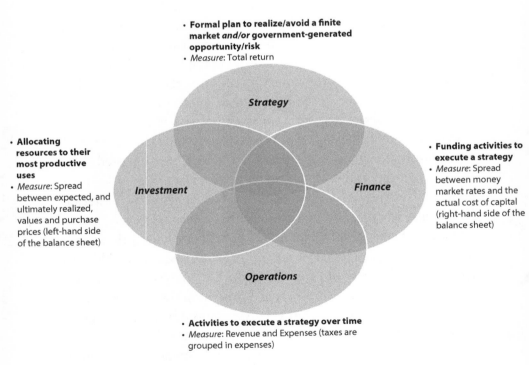

FIGURE 11.2 Jay Gould and Corporate Management. *Source*: Joseph Calandro, Jr.

has continuous high performance for very long periods of time (an achievement that is almost nonexistent) to one that can string together a series of temporary advantages over time."[22]

Furthermore, the basis of a strategy could be either market based and/or government based, such as revenue generated from doing business with the government (including transporting mail over the railroad), obtaining a subsidy from the government (including railroad land grants that were and are very valuable), tax credits, or borrowing money from the government at attractive rates (the UP had several loans from the government before Gould acquired control).[23] For a modern example, consider Elon Musk: at the time of this writing, his companies received $4.9 billion in governmental assistance and a "cheap" $465 million loan from the Department of Energy, and owners of Tesla automobiles receive valuable tax credits. According to one financial analyst, Musk "definitely goes where there is government money."[24]

A measure of strategic success is *total return*, which is defined as the sum of capital appreciation, dividends, interest, and distributions generated over the duration of a strategy.[25] **Figure 11.1** is an indication of the total return Gould's activities generated through the appreciation of UP equity.

Investment pertains to the allocation of scarce resources or factors of production, which are defined as land, labor, capital, and information where "land" encompasses property, plant, and equipment. Investments are recorded on the left-hand side of the balance sheet and are evaluated based on the spread between expected—and ultimately realized—values compared to purchase prices (or historical costs) over time.

Jay Gould was a successful investor, which means he allocated capital to investments that, on average, significantly appreciated in value over time. Long-term investment success is generated from many factors, but a key factor is a healthy dose of contrarianism.[26] A classic book on this subject is *The Art of Contrary Thinking*, which begins this way: "The art of contrary thinking may be stated simply: Thrust your thoughts out of the rut. In a word, be a *non-conformist* when using your mind. . . . Let me give you an easily remembered epigram to sum up this thought: When everyone thinks alike, everyone is likely to be wrong" (emphasis original).[27] The way this definition is worded can lead pretty much anyone to think they are a "contrarian," which of course they are not, for as James Grant has insightfully observed, "What money can't buy—what brains frequently don't contribute—is a precious, non-consensus view of the future."[28] The reason for this is that "accepting the broad concept of contrarianism is one thing; putting it into practice is another."[29] Michael Lewis explains why in *Liar's Poker*:

> Everyone wants to be [a contrarian], but no one is, for the sad reason that most investors are scared of looking foolish.[30] Investors do not fear losing money as much as they fear solitude, by which I mean taking risks others avoid. When they are caught losing money alone, they have no excuse for their mistake, and most investors, like most people, need excuses. They are, strangely enough, happy to stand on the edge of a precipice as long as they are joined by a few thousand others.[31] But when a market is widely regarded to be in a bad way, even if the problems are illusory, many investors get out.[32, 33]

Contrarianism is inherently counter-cyclical for as Benjamin Graham explained: "There are two requirements for success . . . One, you have to think correctly; and secondly, you have to think independently."[34] This distinction is important because most corporate managers and investors within an industry think and move with the cycle, not against it, which is why there is a cycle.

Even the most successful investors are criticized when they act contrary to common perceptions (or counter-cyclically). Consider this example: On November 2, 2009, Berkshire Hathaway announced it was taking Burlington Northern Santa Fe Railroad (Burlington) private in a deal valued at $100 per share, which was approximately 31 percent higher than the share price at the time.[35] Surprisingly, this announcement came under sharp criticism from sources relatively close to Warren Buffett, including his authorized biographer.[36] This deal nevertheless turned out extremely well. As Buffett pointed out in the 2010 Berkshire Hathaway Annual Report: "The highlight of 2010 was our acquisition of Burlington Northern Santa Fe, a purchase that's working out even better than I expected. It now appears that owning this railroad will increase Berkshire's 'normal' earning power by nearly 40 percent pretax and by well over 30 percent after tax. Making this purchase increased our share count by 6 percent and used $22 billion of cash. Since we've quickly replenished the cash, the economics of this transaction have turned out very well."[37] The last two sentences pertain to the financing of the Burlington deal, which segues to our next capability.

Finance pertains to the funding of resources for the duration of a strategic initiative and is recorded on the right-hand side of the balance sheet. Financial acumen is evaluated based on the spread between money market rates and actual financing costs. Despite the relative popularity of corporate finance courses and books, true financial expertise is very rare.[38] One reason for this is likely the academic financial proposition that capital structure is "irrelevant," which has been shown time and again to not be true in real life. In contrast, one of the things that most impresses me about Warren Buffett is the way he has funded his investment activities over his career, as anyone who has viewed a clip of his annual shareholders meetings can readily see.

Operations pertain to the people, processes, and technology that enable strategic execution over time. Operational results are reflected in the income and cash flow statements via a number of revenue, expense, and earnings metrics. Operations tend to be shorter-term focused as measured by revenue and expense line items in contrast to longer-term investments that are recorded on the balance sheet.

Conclusion

Interactive dynamics add a level of complexity to both corporate and investment management, hence the concentric circles in
Figure 11.2.[39] There are technical reasons for this, such as the
well-known principle that financing should economically "match"
both operational and investment needs, but a great deal more
is required to make a corporate manager successful. According
to investment theorist Phil Fisher, one thing that should not be
overlooked is "the general term of integrity [that] encompasses
both the honesty and general decency of those who are running the company."[40] As a corporate manager, Jay Gould was
remarkably humble:

> In meetings he never dominated discussion but let it drone
> on before expressing succinctly and precisely the point oth-
> ers had been groping for. He did not command or dictate but
> suggested politely. Far from being an imperious figure, he was
> content to dwell in the shadows and let others take credit. For
> a man consumed by ambition, he was strikingly unaffected
> by considerations of ego or vanity.[41]

To understand how this framework could be applied, consider
the modern example of share buybacks. As interest rates were
pushed to historically low levels following the 2007–2008 financial
crisis, the cost of debt fell to historically low levels while equity values increased. Many corporate managers viewed this situation as
an opportunity to swap underpriced debt for overvalued equity;[42]
in other words, they derived a strategy to buy back their stock at
attractive financing rates regardless of price levels.[43] Such strategies
have had mixed results.

To understand why, consider the modern railroad industry.
Journalist S. L. Mintz profiled this industry, and one of his findings

was that "for the eight quarters through December 2015, most Class 1 railroads that returned capital to shareholders posted a negative buyback return on investment."[44] In other words, their buybacks resulted in a capital loss. Significantly, the UP was profiled in Mintz's study and reflected a negative 14.8 percent buyback ROI, which contrasts sharply with Gould's 19 percent compounded return, especially considering the macroeconomic environments the two results were produced in: Gould generated a 19 percent compounded annual growth rate while cleaning up the UP's balance sheet during years of depression and deflation while the UP's modern negative buyback ROI was generated during a period of easy money and asset inflation, which is very bullish for equity prices.

I will speculate that if either Jay Gould or Henry Singleton (**Chapter 5**) were alive today, they would not have followed the crowd buying back shares at inflated prices, and their reasons should by now be obvious. This is just one of the lessons reflected in the histories of these successful corporate managers, which should not be rejected until they have been studied and understood, to paraphrase the quote of Benjamin Graham that introduced this chapter.

Conclusion and Information Advantage

"To strive, to seek, to find, and not to yield."
—THE LAST LINE OF TENNYSON'S *ULYSSES*,
WHICH IS ALSO THE LAST LINE OF
BENJAMIN GRAHAM'S MEMOIRS[1]

IN THE INTRODUCTION, we chronicled the celebrated history of value investing and closed our discussion by providing thoughts on what its future could entail, most especially with respect to the application of value investing theory to corporate strategy and management. **Chapter 1** followed by outlining several actions that executives could consider when applying value investing theory to the management of their firms. These actions were summarized in Table C.1, which is reproduced at the top of the next page.

Sound strategy is widely recognized as the foundation of effective corporate management. Successful business strategies articulate value propositions to attract and retain customers, which are different from those of competitors. Value investing corporate management takes strategy a step further by enabling value propositions with the margin of safety principle. **Chapter 2** profiled several ways to accomplish this based on insights derived from Seth Klarman's book of the same name.

When I have discussions on this topic, I get the impression that some executives think this is easy to do, which it most certainly is

Table C.1
Value Investing Corporate Management Considerations

1. Unique value proposition *and* how the margin of safety will enable that proposition
2. How will business activities be funded or financed?
3. Balance:
    a) across operations, finance, and investment
    b) of cyclical and counter-cyclical dynamics as reflected in mainstream *and* alternative information sources
    c) between business-as-usual processes *and* the "thick tails" of nonlinear events to both the upside *and* downside
4. Clarity of communication *and* transparency of expectations
5. Humility
6. Produce results that compound over time

not; in fact, even executives who are well read in value investing theory have failed at it. The reason why should be obvious by now: margin of safety–rich opportunities emerge by thinking and acting in a contrary way to peers, colleagues, most board members, and competitors, and most people are simply not wired to withstand the pressures of truly thinking and acting differently. It is much, much easier to do what everyone else is doing, and buy what everyone else is buying, at prices that everyone else is paying. This is not to say that it is impossible to employ the margin of safety in a corporate setting, only that it is *very* difficult to do so, which is a reason why it is so rare.

The next activity or consideration listed in the above table pertains to funding. Modern financial economics holds that capital structure is "irrelevant," and to be frank, when looking at the broad economy since the early 1980s it is hard to argue with this "proposition."[2] However, on a firm by firm (or microeconomic) basis, many successful value investors consider capital structure the most relevant managerial consideration, second only to strategy.

Highly successful executive managers across time, from Thomas Edison to Steve Jobs, lost control of their companies by not adequately appreciating and/or managing the power and risks of their capital structures. Value investing corporate managers, on the other hand, both understand and intensely manage it. One way they do so is via their cash holdings which, at times, can be considerable. In fact, at certain times, ample cash holdings can serve as a "competitive advantage," which was the theme of **Chapter 3**.

In **Chapter 4**, we expanded our discussion from strategy to corporate management in general. This chapter profiled several value investing corporate management insights derived from the sixth edition of Graham and Dodd's seminal book, *Security Analysis*, as well as an interview on this subject with the lead editor of the book, value investor Seth Klarman.

One major theme of value investing corporate management is "balance," which, broadly defined, means a balanced managerial focus across operations, finance, and investment; across both cyclical and counter-cyclical market dynamics; and across both business-as-usual processes as well as the thick tails of nonlinear opportunities and threats. An example of such management capabilities was profiled in **Chapter 5** via the exploits of the late Henry Singleton of Teledyne. He has been profiled in the value investing literature before, but this chapter takes a more detailed look at what he did *and* how he did it based on research conducted in real time by value investor Lee Cooperman as well as two autobiographies of Singleton's associates.[3] This profile is the first of four detailed case studies included in this book, each of which illustrates a different facet of value investing corporate management in action.

One characteristic that value investing corporate managers exhibit is clarity of communication, which is augmented by a healthy and refreshing dose of personal humility. These behaviors often result in repeatedly "rational" managerial actions where rational is defined as business activities that consistently match stated goals and objectives over time. This is an incredibly powerful and actionable concept, for both corporate and investment managers, as was explained in **Chapter 6.**

Most corporate managers are, understandably, operationally focused. However, and as noted above, the value investing corporate manager balances their focus across operations, finance, and investment activities. The late value investor Marty Whitman was at the forefront of exploring this potent capability, and in **Chapter 7,** we profiled it along with a number of other managerial insights from his book, *Modern Security Analysis*, and from an interview that I conducted with him.

All of these managerial activities coalesce into the realization of significant value—for customers, owners, employees, and other key stakeholders—that compounds powerfully over time. In fact, one can argue that value realization is "The Most Important Thing," as we argued in **Chapter 8,** based on value investor Howard Marks's book of the same name. We then went on to illustrate this concept in action in the last three case studies profiled in this book, which pertained to GEICO, the GTI Corporation, and Jay Gould of the Union Pacific (**Chapters 9, 10, and 11**). Each of these chapters examined a different facet of value realization: the GEICO case profiles a value investing–consistent approach to performance management, the GTI case profiles how an analytical model can be used to realize value, which is an incredibly important and timely topic, and the Union Pacific case profiles the many lessons that can be learned from perhaps the first value investing–consistent corporate manager, the late and much maligned Jay Gould.

At the center of each of the chapters is "information": quantitative, qualitative, and/or behavioral. In other words, the theme of "information advantage," or knowing something that other managers either do not know *or* choose to ignore, runs through this book.[4]

Indeed, in many ways, it is the basis of margin of safety–rich opportunities in that unpopular information generates little buying activity, which often equates to lower pricing. For example, Benjamin Graham founded value investing by focusing on "net-net" stocks—or stocks selling for appreciably less than their net-net value (current assets less *total* liabilities), which were widely ignored by the investors of his day.[5] This dynamic has continued throughout value investing's history and is readily apparent in the four case studies profiled in this book.

Henry Singleton used his historical knowledge of interest rates and business, among other things, to deploy innovative and highly successful financial strategies for the almost three decades that he led Teledyne.

Warren Buffett and Tony Nicely used comprehensive and cohesive performance information to realize significant growth value at GEICO. While this information may seem basic—insurance is based on the well-known law of large numbers, after all—I have been involved in the insurance business for over thirty years and have rarely witnessed such well-structured and insightful managerial information. This lesson can be broadly applied across all industries, even (especially) in this age of "big data."

James LaFleur operationalized the insights of a well-known financial distress model to inform his turnaround management activities at GTI, and in so doing provides a textbook case study on how to practically employ modeled output to realize value for corporate stakeholders.

Finally, Jay Gould drilled down deeply into railroad operations and used the knowledge he acquired, along with his legendary financial and investment acumen, and trader-like approach to strategy, to realize incredible value at the UP despite strong macroeconomic headwinds *and* the absence of any governmental assistance. Indeed, financial pressure from the government ultimately resulted in Gould selling his stake in the UP at a considerable profit.

I cannot overemphasize the importance of an information advantage to long-term success. To illustrate, consider the case of professional baseball. Sabermetrics effectively began in the 1960 and 1970s, but it was hardly used professionally until the Oakland A's began employing it in the early 2000s, as profiled in the book *Moneyball.* The Boston Red Sox, under new ownership led by the legendary ex-trader John Henry, adopted a sabermetric–based approach and subsequently won four World Series championships thereby eviscerating the infamous "Curse of the Bambino." However, even after the Chicago Cubs won the World Series in 2016, under the leadership of Theo Epstein, who also led the Red Sox to their first two World Series titles in 2004 and 2007,[6] not all major league teams vigorously employed sabermetrics. Only after the Houston Astros won the World Series in 2017 did that seem to be rectified.[7]

There are many reasons why broad–based sabermetrics adoption in professional baseball took so long,[8] and they are similar to why so many corporate (and investment) managers stay with the same general information sources and methods of analysis. First, professional managers—like most people—tend to stick with things they know and are comfortable with. Second, professional managers have a common skill set given their educational and employment backgrounds, and capabilities that fall outside of this skill set are easy to ignore and under-appreciate. Third, professional managers have a business to run "today," and thus have limited time available to focus on alternative information that may, or may not, prove useful "today." Fourth, as noted above, people in general are hardwired to seek consensus and therefore the true contrarian— the person who really *does* "think differently"—represents a *very* small percentage of the population.[9] Understandably, such people can find it difficult to climb the corporate ladder into management positions, as we discussed in the **Introduction.**

It was noted earlier that the battle of business performance in the short term is frequently won or lost in business-as-usual environments, but the war over the long term is won in "the tails" by economically mitigating the risk of nonlinear losses while capitalizing on opportunities with nonlinear payoffs. Specifically, only by avoiding nonlinear losses *and* capitalizing on nonlinear payoffs can managers hope to compound the kinds of returns that some of the corporate managers profiled in this book have. To illustrate this point, we will first put a picture to it.

The core of **Figure 1** is the normal distribution that everyone is taught in business school. One issue with the normal distribution is that many (most) real-life probability distributions have thick tails rather than thin ones; hence, the dashed line on each tail of the figure. Nonlinear concave loss and convex payoff distributions are illustrated at the bottom of each tail, which is

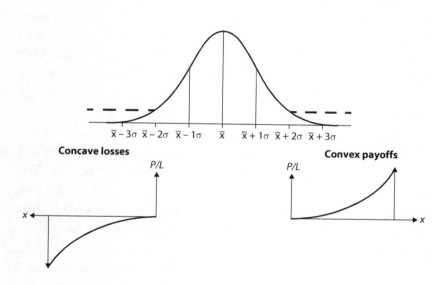

FIGURE 1 Nonlinear Payoffs and Losses—Theory. Convex payoffs (concave losses) can occur in the real economy, the paper/financial economy, and/or the cyber economy. By definition, such payoffs (losses) are both rare and transitory, which is why it is so important to find (avoid) them as much as possible. For more information see Nassim Nicholas Taleb, *Antifragile: Things that Gain from Disorder* (New York: Random House, 2012). I strongly recommend all of Taleb's books and, for those skilled in advanced mathematics, his technical papers.

important because one firm's concave loss can be another's convex payoff. This is one of the reasons why it is so important to vigorously seek out potential nonlinear opportunities and risks using alternative, and often unpopular, information sources. To help demonstrate why, we will revisit an example that was profiled in the **Introduction**.

As you may recall, **Figure 2** illustrates the performance of Prem Watsa of Fairfax Financial Holdings during "the big short" of 2007–2008. Fairfax's performance is on the far right of the exhibit because it had the greatest convex payoff of the six firms that earned such payoffs, which is in stark contrast to all of the firms profiled to the left that incurred concave losses during the same period. In sum, the successful corporate managers (the ones who earned convex payoffs) capitalized on the nonlinear opportunity presented to them prior to "the big short" to both protect their portfolios *and* to economically profit from volatility expansion once it occurred. Ineffective corporate managers, on the other hand, exposed their firms to nonlinear risks and incurred concave losses as a result.

Once again, the war over the long term is frequently won in "the tails" by economically mitigating the risk of concave (or black swan) losses *and* capitalizing on convex (or disruptively innovative) payoffs. Get in the habit of thinking this way. You will be very glad you did, and so will your customers, employees, regulators, investors, and creditors (to the extent you have any), *as long as* you do not erode any potential advantage by prematurely disclosing it.

We live in a world of incessant and all too often useless social media postings and corporate press releases. I have seen a number of potential strategic advantages—and information is one form of strategic advantage, and therefore one basis of a franchise—posted and/or press-released away. Social media posts and press releases are, of course, common sources of information that competitors regularly read. Successful corporate managers do not prematurely

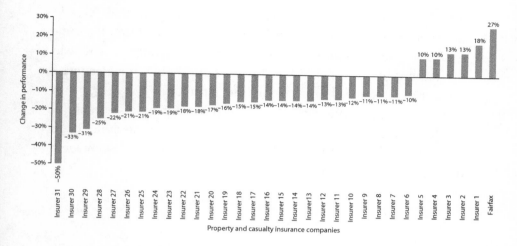

FIGURE 2 Nonlinear Payoffs and Losses—Practice. *Data source*: Dowling & Partners, *IBNR Weekly* #39 (October 5, 2007): 8. The names of the other thirty-one insurers are available from Dowling; I changed the order of the names.

disclose any advantage; rather, like the late Jay Gould, they use the press and, by extension, social media to achieve their strategic goals rather than just "see their name in lights."[10] This may sound like common sense, but that doesn't mean it is common.

In closing, I am often asked for career advice by students, postdocs, and professionals in every stage of their careers. My reply, which references Charlie Munger's famous "three rules for a career,"[11] may therefore be a good way to conclude this book. Munger is, of course, the popular vice-chairman of Berkshire Hathaway.

The first rule is "don't sell anything you wouldn't buy yourself." Consider GEICO: It took a product that most people would like to ignore, automobile insurance, and made it enjoyable, beginning with a highly innovative marketing campaign that facilitated decades of profitable growth.

The second rule is "don't work for anyone you don't respect and admire." After I published the paper that preceded **Chapter 5** of this book, I had the opportunity to speak with several people who had worked for Henry Singleton. To a person, their eyes lit up when they spoke of him, and they all pretty much said the same thing: "He was absolutely brilliant. And he was tough, a real taskmaster, but he was always fair. Most of all, though, he was just a good man." We need more Henry Singletons.[12]

Munger's third rule is to "work only with people you enjoy." As the saying goes, "Life is just too short to be an asshole, or to spend time with assholes."[13] Words to live, work, and manage a business by, and to end a book on.

Acknowledgments

MARIO GABELLI reinstituted the value investing course at Columbia University, which literally got me started in this field. Mario was also a guest speaker in my value investing class at the University of Connecticut when I taught there. He also endorsed my first book, approved my appointment as a Fellow of the Gabelli Center for Global Security Analysis at Fordham University, supported the use of my first book as a supplemental text in the Center's value investing program, and endorsed this book. I owe him a debt of gratitude that I will never be able to repay.

This book would not be possible without Myles Thompson of Columbia University Press. Myles kept after me for years, literally, to write it and for that I sincerely thank him, as well as all of his colleagues who helped bring this book to print, most especially Brian Smith.

I would also like to thank Professor Sris Chatterjee of the Gabelli Center of Global Security Analysis at Fordham University for his very kind **Foreword** to this book. Thanks also to Professor

Jim Kelly, the center's director, for his continued support and friendship. To say that I enjoy working with, and for, both of them would be a gross understatement.

The following people reviewed early drafts of this book and were kind enough to provide endorsements for it, for which I am eternally grateful: Toby Carlisle, Lenny DePaul, Marc Faber, Jeff Gramm, Jim Grant, John Hughes, Mark McNeilly, and Fred Sheehan.

The following people read and/or provided input on the papers that preceded this book and thus helped to make it possible: Ed Altman, Brian Bruce, Lee Cooperman, Fernando Diz, Robert Hagstrom, Seth Klarman, Maury Klein, Howard Marks, Larry Pitkowski, Robert Randall, Jim Schrager, Fred Sheehan, and the late Marty Whitman.

Larry Cunningham, as well as several other reviewers, read early drafts of this book and provided excellent suggestions that helped to make it better, for which I'm very grateful.

Our friends Mark and Debbie Purowitz have supported my work from the start and, more importantly, have always been there when I need a night or two out to clear my head. The word *family* is thrown around a lot these days, but you two really are family.

Thanks to all of my consulting friends and colleagues—especially Greg Galeaz, Francois Ramette, John Sviokla, and Jamie Yoder—for all of their support and encouragement over the years.

Thanks also to my agent, Sheree Bykofsky, for her continued advice, counsel, and representation.

My utmost thanks to my lovely wife and daughter, Terilyn and Alyse, for supporting my somewhat massive book-buying budget and for putting up with all of the bookcases to house my ever-growing collection.

Finally, thanks to my in-laws Larry and Dolores Vecchione, my aunt and uncle Carol and the late Bruce Bickley, my uncle and aunt Jim and Linda Wilson, and the rest of my family for graciously allowing me time on evenings, weekends, and holidays to conduct my research and write.

Notes

Introduction

This introduction contains material from *Financial History*, © 2014 by the Museum of American Finance, which is reprinted with permission. The author would like to thank Frederick J. Sheehan, Jr., for co-authoring the paper that preceded this introduction and Lawrence A. Cunningham for extremely helpful comments and suggestions. Any errors or omissions are solely my fault.

1. Jason Zweig and Rodney Sullivan, ed., *Benjamin Graham Building a Profession* (New York: McGraw-Hill, 2010), 271.

2. Warren Buffett stated in the *1996 Berkshire Hathaway Annual Report*, "In our view, though, investment students need only two well-taught courses—How to Value a Business, and How to Think About Market Prices," http://www.berkshirehathaway.com/letters/1996.html.

3. Joseph Calandro, Jr., "Graham and Dodd: A Perspective on its Past, Present and Possible Future," *Journal of Investing* 22, no. 1 (2014): 7–16.

4. Bruce C. N. Greenwald, et al., *Value Investing: From Graham to Buffett and Beyond* (New York: Wiley, 2001), 159.

5. For more information on Neff see John Neff and S. L. Mintz, *John Neff on Investing* (New York: Wiley, 1999).

6. Michael Lewis, *The Big Short: Inside the Doomsday Machine* (New York: Norton, 2010), 105.

7. Benjamin Graham and David Dodd, *Security Analysis*, 2nd ed. (New York: McGraw-Hill, 1940 [1934]), 596.

8. For two well–known value–based examples see David Einhorn, *Fooling Some of the People All of the Time* (Hoboken, NJ: Wiley, 2008), and Christine Richard, *Confidence Game: How a Hedge Fund Manager Called Wall Street's Bluff* (Hoboken, NJ: Wiley, 2010).

Appendix: Common Ground and/or Areas of Further Research

1. Bruce Greenwald, preface to *Value Investing: From Graham to Buffett and Beyond*, by Bruce C. N. Greenwald, et al. (New York: Wiley, 2001), ix.

2. Willard Sterne Randall, *Alexander Hamilton: A Life* (New York: HarperCollins, 2003), 385–95, and Thomas DiLorenzo, chapter 2 in *Hamilton's Curse* (New York: Crown, 2008).

3. David Nasaw, *Andrew Carnegie* (New York: Penguin, 2006), 141.

4. *Financial Crisis Inquiry Commission Staff Audiotape of Interview with Warren Buffett, Berkshire Hathaway*, transcript provided by *Santangel's Review*, May 26, 2010, 6.

5. James Grant, "To the Gnomes of Zurich," *Grant's Interest Rate Observer* 37, no. 7 (April 5, 2019): 1.

6. Seth A. Klarman, "Preface to the Sixth Edition: The Timeless Wisdom of Graham and Dodd," in Benjamin Graham and David Dodd, *Security Analysis*, 6th ed. (New York: McGraw-Hill, 2009 [1934]), xxiv. According to *Investopedia*, "The company [Enron] paid its creditors more than $21.7 billion from 2004 to 2011. Its last payout was in May 2011" (Enron Scandal, https://www.investopedia.com/updates/enron-scandal-summary/).

7. Which include the distressed claims of Madoff investors. For more information see Nathan Vardi, "The Great Baupost Madoff Claim Trade That Made a Big Madoff Feeder Fund a Loser Again," *Forbes*, (January 16, 2013), http://www.forbes.com/sites/nathanvardi/2013/01/16/the-great-baupost -madoff-claims-trade-that-made-a-big-madoff-feeder-fund-a-loser-again/. For information on how this distressed investment turned out, see Erik Larson and Christopher Cannon, "Madoff's Victims Are Close to Getting Their $19 Billion Back," *Bloomberg* (December 8, 2018), https://www .bloomberg.com/graphics/2018-recovering-madoff-money/.

8. Joseph Calandro, Jr., and Francois Ramette, "An Underwriting Approach to Estimating the Cost of Property & Casualty Equity," *Journal of*

Insurance and Financial Management 2, no. 8 (2016): 98–111. The working paper can be found here at SSRN: https://ssrn.com/abstract=2826596.

9. The modern trend of excessive debt-financed government spending began with "The Gipper" as powerfully told by David Stockman, *The Triumph of Politics: How the Reagan Revolution Failed* (New York: Harper & Row, 1986).

10. James Grant, "Risk and Reward," *Grant's Interest Rate Observer* 37, no. 9 (May 3, 2019): 9.

11. Grant, "Risk and Reward," 9.

12. Sadly, this was not the first time that I have heard such a thing.

13. Katherine Doherty, "Father of Z-Score Expects Bigger Bankruptcies in Next Downturn," *Bloomberg*, November 12, 2018, https://www.bloomberg .com/news/articles/2018-11-09/father-of-z-score-sees-bigger-bankruptcies-in -next-downturn-q-a.

14. For my thoughts on systemic risk see, Joseph Calandro, Jr., "Systemic Risk and Risk Management: Overview and Approach," *Journal of Insurance and Financial Management*, 2, no. 8 (2016): 1–35. The working paper can be found at SSRN: https://ssrn.com/abstract=2815616.

15. See also Gregory Zuckerman, *The Greatest Trade Ever* (New York: Broadway, 2009).

1. Value Investing and Corporate Management: Overview

1. Irving Kahn and Robert Milne, *Benjamin Graham: The Father of Financial Analysis* (Charlottesville, VA: Financial Analysts Research Foundation, 1977), 1.

2. Glenn Greenberg, "The Quest for Rational Investing," in Benjamin Graham and David Dodd, *Security Analysis*, 6th ed. (New York: McGraw-Hill, 2009), 401. For my interpretation of value investing general principles see Joseph Calandro, Jr., *Value Investing General Principles* (September 21, 2016), available at SSRN: https://ssrn.com/abstract=2575429.

3. General principle #1 per Calandro (2016), cited immediately above.

4. The data used in the example is from top-tier value investing funds with established long-term track records whose names I cannot divulge.

5. Cboe Advanced Quotes, http://www.cboe.com/delayedquote/advanced -charts?ticker=VIX (accessed 12 February 2018).

6. Cboe Advanced Quotes.

7. Joseph Calandro, Jr., "A Leader's Guide to Strategic Risk Management," *Strategy & Leadership* 43, no. 1 (2015): 26–35.

8. As of the date of this writing (late-2018), volatility has dissipated in the VIX, and thus I am once again speaking to it as a possible economical hedge to select clients; however, many struggle to see the benefits of such "insurance" in a capital markets context, which is an experience not unique to me. For more information see Michelle Celarier, "How Jim Chanos Uses Cynicism, Chutzpah—and a Secret Twitter Account—to Take on Markets (and Elon Musk)," *Institutional Investor*, September 17, 2018, https://www .institutionalinvestor.com/article/b1b00ynrgtn05r/How-Jim-Chanos-Uses -Cynicism-Chutzpah-and-a-Secret-Twitter-Account-to-Take-on-Markets -and-Elon-Musk.

9. Buffett has courted, and stayed in the good graces of, government, which has enabled him to avoid the regulatory issues that plagued Rockefeller. While this strategy has been incredibly successful, it is interestingly not consistent with the philosophy of his libertarian father, the late, great congressman Howard Buffett.

10. For information on Rockefeller, see Ron Chernow, *Titan: The Life of John D. Rockefeller* (New York: Random House, 1998).

11. Corporate managers who get both sides of their balance sheets working together over time are able to generate "cash feedback." For more information see Joseph Calandro, Jr., "The 'Next Phase' of Strategic Acquisition," *The Journal of Private Equity* (Winter 2015): 32–33.

12. On black swans see Nassim N. Taleb, *The Black Swan: The Impact of the Highly Improbable* (New York: Random House, 2007). As the late Andy Grove observed, "The ability to recognize that the winds have shifted and to take appropriate action before you wreck your boat is crucial to the future of an enterprise." *Only the Paranoid Survive: How to Exploit the Crisis Points that Challenge Every Company* (New York: Currency, 1999 [1996]), 21.

13. "Individuals talk and write a good deal about resolving major, long-term issues, but in fact most of their activities consist of dealing as best they can with specific, limited, often mundane, short-range problems." Robert Sobel, *The Fallen Colossus: The Great Crash of The Penn Central* (New York: Beard, 2000 [1977]), 163.

14. Note also Mark McNeilly, *Sun Tzu and the Art of Business: Six Strategic Principles for Managers*, rev. ed. (New York: Oxford, 2012 [1996]).

15. "Humanity is the quality which stops one being arrogant towards one's fellows, or being acrimonious." Robin Alexander Campbell, tr., Seneca, *Letters from a Stoic* (New York: Penguin, 2014 [1969]), 177–78.

16. The seminal book on the reevaluation of President Eisenhower is Fred Greenstein, *The Hidden Hand Presidency: Eisenhower as Leader* (New York: Basic Books, 1982).

17. As David Stockman explains in *The Great Deformation: The Corruption of Capitalism in America* (New York: PublicAffairs, 2013):

> In the final analysis, Eisenhower's fiscal record is one of a kind. Between fiscal 1953 and 1961, total federal spending declined from 20.4 percent of GDP to 18.4 percent. The constant-dollar federal budget was reduced from about $680 billion to $650 billion.
>
> Never again did the nation's inflation-adjusted budget number shrink during a presidential term. . . .
>
> In contrast to the decline in constant-dollar federal spending during Eisenhower's tenure, real outlays during the three subsequent surges of warfare state spending rose steeply. The Kennedy–Johnson period recorded an increase of 50 percent, while the eight Reagan years saw inflation-adjusted growth in total federal spending of 22 percent.
>
> The all-time record was achieved during the George W. Bush presidency, of course, when constant-dollar federal spending expanded by an even greater 53 percent (218–19).

For information on President Eisenhower's fiscal policies see William McClenahan, Jr., and William Becker, *Eisenhower and the Cold War Economy* (Baltimore, MD: Johns Hopkins, 2011).

18. As John S. D. Eisenhower observed in *General Ike: A Personal Reminiscence* (New York: Free Press, 2003), "The words 'humility must be the portion . . .' are among Ike's immortal expressions of the role of the commander" (223). Note also Carlo D'Este, *Eisenhower: A Soldier's Life* (New York: Hold and Co., 2002).

19. There is a difference between political parties and governmental functions. While some governmental functions are, shall we say, less than efficient, others are incredibly well run. One example is the U.S. Marshals Service, which is tasked with—amongst other things—bringing the most dangerous fugitives to justice. They successfully accomplish this mission year after year with little to no fanfare, unlike some other law enforcement agencies. For more information on the Marshals Service, and the lessons that can be applied to corporate management, see Lenny DePaul, Joseph Calandro, Jr., and Eric Trowbridge, "What Corporate Executives Can Learn from the U.S. Marshals Service," *American Security Today* 17 (October 2017): 17–27, https://americansecuritytoday.com/corporate-executives-can-learn-u-s-marshals-service/. The corresponding research paper is Lenny DePaul and Joseph Calandro, Jr., *Strategy Through Execution: Lessons from the U.S. Marshals* (October 4, 2017) [September 25 (2017)], available at SSRN: https://ssrn.com/abstract=3042577.

20. James Grant, "Business Is Hard," *Grant's Interest Rate Observer* 34, no. 6 (March 25, 2016): 11.

21. Chris Schelling, "The 'No Jerks' Rule of Investing," *Institutional Investor*, September 13, 2018, https://www.institutionalinvestor.com/article /b19y8b1zzmx8kx/The-No-Jerks-Rule-of-Investing?utm_medium=email&utm _campaign=The%20Essential%20II%20091418&utm_content=The%20 Essential%20II%20091418%20CID_86dca1384b9d910c6a1f246fd64e7 796&utm_source=CampaignMonitorEmail&utm_term=The%20No%20 Jerks%20Rule%20of%20Investing.

2. Corporate Strategy and the "Margin of Safety"

This chapter contains material from *Strategy & Leadership*, © 2011 by Emerald Publishing, which is reprinted with permission. The author would like to thank Seth A. Klarman for helpful questions, comments, and suggestions on earlier drafts of this chapter. Any errors or omissions are solely my fault.

1. Benjamin Graham and Spencer Meredith, *The Interpretation of Financial Statements* (New York: Harper & Row, 1998 [1937]), 77.

2. Seth A. Klarman, "The Timeless Wisdom of Graham and Dodd," in Benjamin Graham and David Dodd, *Security Analysis*, 6th ed. (New York: McGraw-Hill, 2009), xxxv.

3. *Berkshire Hathaway Annual Report, 1992*, http://www.berkshirehathaway .com/letters/1992.html.

4. Seth A. Klarman, *Margin of Safety: Risk-Adverse Value Investing Strategies for the Thoughtful Investor* (New York: HarperBusiness, 1991), 94.

5. Walter Kiechel, chapters 3 and 11 in *The Lords of Strategy: The Secret Intellectual History of the New Corporate World* (Boston, MA: HBS Press, 2010). Also note Bruce Henderson's comment: "Cost effectiveness analysis optimizes value relative to cost," in *The Logic of Business Strategy* (Cambridge, MA: Ballinger, 1984), 25. He goes on to state, "Strategic sector analysis optimizes margin relative to competition" (25).

6. Zachary Mider, "New Deal Rush Pushes Takeovers to Most Expensive Since Lehman," *Bloomberg*, March 30, 2011, http://www.bloomberg .com/news/2011-03-30/new-deal-rush-pushes-takeovers-to-most-expensive -since-lehman.html. Such behavior continues to the time of this writing (mid-2018): Lucy White, "Global Deal Values Are Expected to Hit a Record High in the First Half of 2018, as the Total Has Already Bombed Through $1.7bn," *CITY A.M.*, May 4, 2018, http://www.cityam.com/285307/global -deal-values-expected-hit-record-high-first-half-2018.

7. Similar behavior continues to the time of this writing (mid-2018): Ryan Derousseau, "Why Stock Market Buybacks Should Make Investors Nervous," *Fortune*, April 20, 2018, http://fortune.com/2018/04/20/stock-market-buybacks-nervous/.

8. Note Warren Buffett's comments in the *Berkshire Hathaway Annual Report, 2010*, 21–22.

9. "Individuals talk and write a good deal about resolving major, long-term issues, but in fact most of their activities consist of dealing as best they can with specific, limited, often mundane, short-range problems." Robert Sobel, *The Fallen Colossus: The Great Crash of the Penn Central* (New York: Beard, 2000), 163.

10. For example, note the last paragraph of Dana Mattioli and Chana Schoenberger, "For Some, Currency Hedging Is No Gain," *Wall Street Journal*, February 19, 2011, http://online.wsj.com/article/SB10001424052748703803904576152442756363116.html.

11. Charles Stein, "Klarman Tops Griffin as Hedge-Fund Investors Hunt for 'Margin of Safety,'" *Bloomberg*, June 11, 2010, http://www.bloomberg.com/news/2010-06-11/klarman-tops-griffin-as-hedge-fund-investors-hunt-for-margin-of-safety-.html.

12. Michael Lewis, *The Big Short: Inside the Doomsday Machine* (New York: Norton, 2010), 105.

13. Franco Modigliani and Merton Miller, "The Cost of Capital, Corporation Finance and the Theory of Investment," *The American Economic Review*, 48, no. 3 (June 1958): 261–97. Subsequent works qualified the extent of irrelevance, but the theory remains a staple of finance to this day. See, for example, Donald MacKenzie, *An Engine, Not a Camera: How Financial Models Shape Markets* (Cambridge, MA: MIT, 2006).

14. Lawrence McDonald and Patrick O'Brien, *A Colossal Failure of Common Sense: The Inside Story of the Collapse of Lehman Brothers* (New York: Crown, 2009), 263. The authors note, "There is an army of eagle-eyed hedge funds on the lookout for misplaced hubris and out-of-touch management, especially when there's crushing debt" (224).

15. Lewis, *The Big Short*, 174; Gregory Zuckerman, *The Greatest Trade Ever: The Behind-the-Scenes Story of How John Paulson Defied Wall Street and Made Financial History* (New York: Broadway, 2009), 256.

16. Bruce Greenwald, "Deconstructing the Balance Sheet," in Graham and Dodd (2009), 539.

17. Klarman, *Margin of Safety*, 91.

18. William E. Fruhan, Jr., "Corporate Raiders: Head'em Off at Value Gap," *Harvard Business Review* (July–August 1998): 63.

19. Joseph Calandro, Jr., "A Leader's Guide to Strategic Risk Management," *Strategy & Leadership*, 43, no. 1 (2015): 26–35.

20. L. J. Rittenhouse, *Investing Between the Lines: How to Make Smarter Decisions by Decoding CEO Communications* (New York: McGraw-Hill, 2013).

21. Pankaj Ghemawat, chapter 5 in *Commitment: The Dynamic of Strategy* (New York: Free Press, 1991), found that competitive advantages tend to have average life expectancies of approximately ten years.

22. Henderson, *The Logic of Business Strategy*, 104.

23. Karen Hopper Wruck, "Financial Policy as a Catalyst for Organizational Change—Sealed Air's Leveraged Special Dividend," *Journal of Applied Corporate Finance* (Winter 1995): 21.

24. Andrew Grove, chapter 5 in *Only the Paranoid Survive: How to Exploit the Crisis Points that Challenge Every Company* (New York: Currency: 1999).

25. For more information on resource conversion see Martin J. Whitman and Fernando Diz, chapter 22 in *Modern Security Analysis: Understanding Wall Street Fundamentals* (Hoboken, NJ: Wiley, 2013).

26. Rittenhouse, *Investing Between the Lines.*

27. Similarly, Intel cofounder Bob Noyce was concerned with markets that "would unrealistically inflate the firm's market cap." Leslie Berlin, *The Man Behind the Microchip: Robert Noyce and the Invention of Silicon Valley* (New York: Oxford, 2005), 179.

28. *Berkshire Hathaway Owners' Manual*, http://www.berkshirehathaway .com/ownman.pdf, 4.

29. "Starbursting: Breaking Up Companies Is Back in Fashion," *The Economist*, March 24, 2011, http://www.economist.com/node/18440915. An example at the time of this writing (mid-2018) is "VW Weighs Spinoffs of Noncore Assets," *Automotive News*, May 3, 2018, http://www.autonews.com /article/20180503/COPY01/305039980/vw-weighs-spinoffs-of-noncore-assets.

30. Tom Copeland, Tim Koller, and Jack Murrin, *Valuation: Measuring and Managing the Value of Companies*, 3rd ed. (New York: Wiley, 2000 [1990]), 160–61. According to Ghemawat (1991), strategy "is concerned with what seems to be the real locus of action: the numerator of DCF [or discounted cash flow] analysis" (72).

31. Lynn Thomasson and Whitney Kisling, "CEOs Tap Record $940 Billion Cash for Dividends as M&A at Post-Lehman High," *Bloomberg*, March 28, 2011, http://www.bloomberg.com/news/2011-03-27/ceos-tap -record-940-billion-cash-for-dividends-as-m-a-at-post-lehman-high.html. In contrast, "J. P. Morgan never left the office for the day without looking over the entries in the daily ledger, particularly the firm's cash balance.

Nothing concerned him more than the need to maintain liquidity." Vincent P. Carosso, *The Morgans: Private International Bankers 1854–1913* (Cambridge, MA: Harvard University Press, 1987), 437.

32. Klarman, *Margin of Safety*, 109. For a contrary opinion see, for example, Gary Smith, "Apple's Share Buyback Is a Smarter Use of Its Cash than These 4 Other Options," *MarketWatch*, May 7, 2018, https://www .marketwatch.com/story/apples-share-buyback-is-a-smarter-use-of-its-cash -than-these-4-other-options-2018-05-07. It is important to understand that value investors usually operate contrary to conventional wisdom and business-as-usual processes. For more information see Joseph Calandro, Jr., *Value Investing General Principles*, September 21, 2016, available at SSRN: https:// ssrn.com/abstract=2575429.

33. "Profile of Seth Klarman & Baupost Group," *Marketfolly*, June 11, 2010, http://www.marketfolly.com/2010/06/profile-of-seth-klarman-baupost -group_11.html, and "Absolute Return Interviews Seth Klarman," *Greenbackd*, June 7, 2010, http://greenbackd.com/2010/06/07/absolute-return-interviews -seth-klarman/.

34. Christopher Winans, *The King of Cash: The Inside Story of Laurence Tisch* (New York: Wiley, 1995), 6.

35. *Berkshire Hathaway Annual Report, 2010,* http://www.berkshire hathaway.com/letters/2010ltr.pdf.

36. Klarman, *Margin of Safety*, xix.

37. Klarman, *Margin of Safety*, xix.

38. James Grant, "I Can't Believe They're Covenants!" *Grant's Interest Rate Observer* 36, no. 9 (May 4, 2018): 4.

39. Klarman, *Margin of Safety*, 39.

40. Klarman, *Margin of* Safety, 109.

41. Klarman, *Margin of Safety*, xxxviii–xxxix.

42. Klarman, *Margin of Safety*, xviii.

43. Klarman, *Margin of Safety*, 125.

44. Klarman, *Margin of Safety*, 146.

3. Cash and Competitive Advantage

This chapter contains material from *Strategy & Leadership*, © 2015 by Emerald Publishing, which is reprinted with permission. The author would like to thank Robert Randall for helpful questions, comments, and suggestions on earlier drafts of this chapter. Any errors or omissions are solely my fault.

1. Benjamin Graham and Spencer Meredith, *The Interpretation of Financial Statements* (New York: Harper & Row, 1998), 31.

2. James Grant, *Mr. Market Miscalculates: The Bubble Years and Beyond* (Mt. Jackson, VA: Axios, 2008), 91.

3. Jean Tirole, *The Theory of Corporate Finance* (Princeton, NJ: Princeton, 2006), 51.

4. Graham and Meredith, *The Interpretation of Financial Statements*, 31.

5. Joe S. Bain, *Barriers to New Competition: Their Character and Consequences in Manufacturing Industries* (Cambridge, MA: Harvard University Press, 1956), 55.

6. Which I am dating from 1979 based on the following seminal work: William E. Fruhan, Jr., *Financial Strategy: Studies in the Creation, Transfer, and Destruction of Shareholder Value* (Homewood, IL: Irwin, 1979).

7. Tom Copeland, Tim Koller and Jack Murrin, *Valuation: Measuring and Managing the Value of Companies*, 3rd ed. (New York: Wiley, 2000), 160–61. Interestingly, this work was published around the peak of the "new economy" boom. As Marc Faber, *Tomorrow's Gold: Asia's Age of Discovery* (New York: CSLA, 2010 [2002]), observed, "During every manic [business cycle] phase . . . cash is always regarded as a totally unattractive investment alternative. Actually, there is frequently a panic out of cash" (138).

8. "Companies that become troubled almost always suffer from a cash shortage." Martin J. Whitman and Fernando Diz, *Distress Investing: Principles and Technique* (Hoboken, NJ: Wiley, 2009), 121.

9. Nicholas Dunbar, *Inventing Money: The Story of Long-Term Capital Management and the Legends Behind It* (New York: Wiley, 2000), 181, 188, and 190.

10. Martin Mayer, *The Fed: The Inside Story of How the World's Most Powerful Financial Institution Drives the Markets* (New York: Free Press, 2001), 103.

11. Joseph Calandro, Jr., "A Leader's Guide to Strategic Risk Management," *Strategy & Leadership* 43, no. 1 (2015): 26–35. By way of background, from the famous Panic of 1907 until the present day, there has generally been at least one contagious financial event every ten years or so. For more information on the Panic of 1907, see Robert Bruner and Sean Carr, *The Panic of 1907: Lessons Learned from the Market's Perfect Storm* (Hoboken, NJ: Wiley, 2007).

12. According to Stuart C. Gilson, *Creating Value Through Corporate Restructuring: Case Studies in Bankruptcies, Buyouts, and Breakups* (New York: Wiley, 2001):

> Corporate restructuring is no longer a rare or episodic event that happens to someone else. It has become a common and significant event in the

professional lives of many [corporate] managers. The reach of corporate restructuring is far greater than this when one also considers the web of relationships between restructured companies and their customers, suppliers, lenders, employees, and competitors. And restructuring directly impacts the millions of investors who provide capital to these firms (3).

13. Forced selling has been a characteristic of all American financial crises since the first one in 1819. For information on that crisis see Murray Rothbard, *The Panic of 1819: Reactions and Policies* (Auburn, AL: Mises Institute, 2007 [1962]). According to the late Professor Rothbard, "The financial panic [of 1819] led, as did later panics, to a great scramble for a cash position, and an eagerness to sell stocks of goods at even sacrifice rates" (19). This also applied during the recession of 1920–1921 as witnessed by William Durant's forced or distressed sale of GM to the du Ponts and J. P. Morgan. For more information see Ron Chernow, *The House of Morgan: What You Can Learn from the Most Inexcusable Business Failures of the Last 25 Years* (New York: Atlantic, 1990), 224.

14. "Both the use of debt to fund acquisitions and the ensuing difficulty of servicing debt during downturns have been recurring trends in American economic life." Bruce Wasserstein, *Big Deal: 2000 and Beyond* (New York: Warner, 2000), 70.

15. Lawrence G. McDonald and Patrick Robinson, *A Colossal Failure of Common Sense: The Inside Story of the Collapse of Lehman Brothers* (New York: Crown, 2009), 287–88. Even Lehman Brothers's excessive leverage pales in comparison to LTCM's in 1998. For example, according to Roger Lowenstein, *When Genius Failed: The Rise and Fall of Long-Term Capital Management* (New York: Random House, 2000), "even omitting derivatives, its leverage was greater than 100 to 1" (191).

16. "The philosophical premise of value investing is that the future is unpredictable. Not knowing, and knowing that one can't know, the careful investor insists on a margin of safety in the form of a low price." James Grant, *Mr. Market Miscalculates: The Bubble Years and Beyond* (Mt. Jackson, VA: Axios, 2008), 353.

17. Lowenstein, *When Genius Failed*, 156.

18. Clayton Rose and David Lane, *Going to the Oracle: Goldman Sachs, September 2008*, HBS case services #9-309-069 (June 21, 2011), and Clayton Rose and Sally Canter Ganzfried, *Teaching Note—Going to the Oracle: Goldman Sachs, September 2008*, HBS case services #5-312-045 (August 24, 2011).

19. Roger Lowenstein, *Buffett: The Making of an American Capitalist* (New York: Broadway, 2001 [1995]), 154.

20. Christopher Winans, *The King of Cash: The Inside Story of Laurence Tisch* (New York: Wiley, 1995), 75. See also page 203 regarding how Mr. Tisch applied this strategy to CBS; namely, "he was strengthening CBS's finances so the company could survive in any kind of weather, and he was building a war chest [of cash] that could be cracked open when assets that made sense for CBS could be had for bargain prices."

21. Joseph L. Bower, *Loews Corporation: Corporate Strategy as a Portfolio*, HBS case services #9-309-004 (March 21, 2014), 5.

22. For an economic analysis of both panics, as well as the panics that proceeded them, see Elmus Wicker, *Banking Panics of the Gilded Age* (New York: Cambridge University Press, 2006 [2000]).

23. Harold van Cleveland and Thomas Huertas, *Citibank: 1812–1970* (Cambridge, MA: Harvard, 1985), 52.

24. van Cleveland and Huertas, *Citibank*, 52.

25. Felix Salmon, "Recipe for Disaster: The Formula That Killed Wall Street," *Wired*, February 23, 2009, http://archive.wired.com/techbiz/it/magazine/1703/wp_quant?currentPage=all. On the role of technology in quantitative finance see, for example, Emanuel Derman, *My Life as a Quant: Reflections on Physics and Finance* (Hoboken, NJ: Wiley, 2004), 165, 169, 206, and 212.

26. Grant, *Mr. Market Miscalculates*, 91.

27. Roddy Boyd, *Fatal Risk: A Cautionary Tale of AIG's Corporate Suicide* (Hoboken, NJ: Wiley, 2011), 281.

28. Mark Robichaux, *Cable Cowboy: John Malone and the Rise of the Modern Cable Business* (Hoboken, NJ: Wiley, 2002), 75.

29. Inspired by John C. Camillus, "Strategy as a Wicked Problem," *Harvard Business Review*, May 2008: 1–9.

30. "We should be anticipating not merely all that commonly happens but all that is conceivably capable of happening, if we do not want to be overwhelmed and struck numb by rare events as if they were unprecedented ones; fortune needs envisioning in a thoroughly comprehensive way." Robin Alexander Campbell, tr., Seneca, *Letters from a Stoic* (New York: Penguin, 2014), 206.

31. A wise use of cash, according to Ray Dalio, the head of Bridgewater Associates—the world's largest hedge fund—is to capitalize on economical investments during periods of distress. Morgan Housel, "The Investing Lesson of 1937: Hold Some Cash," *Wall Street Journal*, March 27, 2015, http://www.wsj.com/articles/the-investing-lesson-of-1937-hold-some-cash-1427464147.

32. Thus, ample cash holdings are sometimes used as a takeover screen. For an example, see "Identifying Takeover Targets," *Money-Zine*, March 16, 2015, http://www.money-zine.com/investing/stocks/identifying-takeover-targets/.

4. Corporate Management and "Security Analysis"

This chapter contains material from *Strategy & Leadership*, © 2009 by Emerald Publishing, which is reprinted with permission. The author would like to thank Seth A. Klarman for helpful questions, comments, and suggestions on earlier drafts of this chapter. Any error or omission is solely my fault.

1. Benjamin Graham and David Dodd, *Security Analysis* (New York: McGraw-Hill, 1934), 515.

2. Seth A. Klarman, "Preface to the Sixth Edition: The Timeless Wisdom of Graham and Dodd," in Benjamin Graham and David Dodd, *Security Analysis*, 6th ed. (New York: McGraw-Hill, 2009), xiii–xiv.

3. Robert Lenzer, "Warren Buffett's Idea of Heaven: 'I Don't Have to Work with People I Don't Like,'" *Forbes*, October 18, 1993, 43.

4. For more information see Joseph Calandro, Jr., chapters 2–4 in *Applied Value Investing* (New York: McGraw-Hill, 2009).

5. For more information see Howard Marks, "Unshackling Bonds," in Graham and Dodd (2009), 123–40.

6. For more information see L. J. Rittenhouse, *Investing Between the Lines: How to Make Smarter Decisions by Decoding CEO Communications* (New York: McGraw-Hill, 2013).

7. For more information see James Grant, "Benjamin Graham and *Security Analysis:* The Historical Backdrop," in Graham and Dodd (2009), 1–19.

8. For more information see Thomas Russo, "Globetrotting with Graham and Dodd," in Graham and Dodd (2009), 720–21.

9. For more information see David Abrams, "The Great Illusion of the Stock Market and the Future of Value Investing," in Graham and Dodd (2009), 617–32.

10. Klarman, "Preface to the Sixth Edition: The Timeless Wisdom of Graham and Dodd," xiii–xliv.

11. Grant, "Benjamin Graham and *Security Analysis:* The Historical Backdrop," 1–19.

12. Howard Marks, "Unshackling Bonds," in Graham and Dodd (2009), 123–40.

13. Bruce Greenwald, "Deconstructing the Balance Sheet," in Graham and Dodd (2009), 535–47.

14. Roger Lowenstein, "The Essential Lessons," in Graham and Dodd (2009), 39–60; Roger Lowenstein, *Buffett—The Making of an American Capitalist* (New York: Broadway, 1995).

15. "Investors can be sure of nothing so much as the need to find a margin of safety." James Grant, *Mr. Market Miscalculates: The Bubble Years and Beyond* (Mt. Jackson, VA: Axios, 2008), 302.

16. Warren Buffett, "The Superinvestors or Graham-and-Doddsville," in Benjamin Graham, *The Intelligent Investor*, 4th ed. (New York: Harper & Row, 1973 [1949]), 297–98.

17. See, for example, Paul Carroll and Chunka Mui, *Billion Dollar Lessons: What You Can Learn from the Most Inexcusable Business Failures of the Last 25 Years* (New York: Portfolio, 2008), 62–63.

18. Lowenstein, "The Essential Lessons," 45–47.

19. Pat Dorsey, *What Would Warren Do?* November 11, 2008, CNN, http://money.cnn.com/2008/11/05/pf/warren_buffett.moneymag/index.htm.

20. John Train, *The Money Masters: Nine Great Investors, Their Winning Strategies and How You Can Apply Them* (New York: HarperBusiness, 1994 [1980]), 24.

21. Klarman, "Preface to the Sixth Edition: The Timeless Wisdom of Graham and Dodd," xxxi–xxxii.

5. Value Creating Corporate Management: Henry E. Singleton

This chapter contains material from *Strategy & Leadership*, © 2010 by Emerald Publishing, which is reprinted with permission. The author would like to thank Leon G. Cooperman for helpful questions, comments, and suggestions on earlier drafts of this chapter. Any error or omission is solely my fault.

1. John Train, *The Money Masters: Nine Great Investors, Their Winning Strategies and How You Can Apply Them* (New York: HarperBusiness, 1994), 25.

2. James Grant, *Mr. Market Miscalculates: The Bubble Years and Beyond* (Mt. Jackson, VA: Axios, 2008), 4.

3. Clayton Christensen showed the power of innovative (and disruptive) technologies in his seminal *The Innovator's Dilemma* (New York: HarperBusiness, 2000 [1997]).

4. George Roberts and Robert Vickers, *Distant Force: A Memoir of the Teledyne Corporation and the Man Who Created It* (self-published by Roberts, 2007), 100, 267.

5. Michael Lewis, *The Big Short: Inside The Doomsday Machine* (New York: Norton, 2010), 174.

6. Leon G. Cooperman, "An Open Letter to the Editor of Business Week," *Goldman Sachs*, May 25, 1982, 7.

7. For information on Jimmy Ling, see Robert Sobel, chapter 3 in *Dangerous Dreamers: The Financial Innovators from Charles Merrill to Michael Milken* (New York: Wiley, 1993).

8. Roberts and Vickers, *Distant Force*, 8. For information on the mentioned firms see, for example, John Brooks, *The Go-Go Years: The Drama and Crashing Finale of Wall Street's Bullish 60s* (New York: Allworth, 1998 [1973]).

9. Roberts and Vickers, *Distant Force*, 100.

10. Roberts and Vickers, *Distant Force*, v. See also James Grant, "From Bear to Bull," *Wall Street Journal*, September 19, 2009, http://online.wsj.com/article/SB10001424052970204518504574420811475582956.html, and note the following thoughts of the late Prussian military strategist Helmuth von Moltke (the elder):

> Strategy is a system of *ad hoc* expedients; it is more than knowledge, it is the application of knowledge to practical life, the development of an original idea in accordance with continually changing circumstances. It is the art of action under the pressure of the most difficult conditions.

> Source: Caleb Carr, "The Man of Silence," *The Quarterly Journal of Military History* 1, no. 3 (Spring 1989): 114.

11. Roberts and Vickers, *Distant Force*, 173–74.

12. Roberts and Vickers, *Distant Force*, 63. This was also a lesson that Lt. Gen. William Pagonis learned early in his career as he recalled in *Moving Mountains: Lessons in Leadership and Logistics from the Gulf War* (Boston, MA: Harvard Business School Press, 1992):

> You have to be involved in every aspect of an organization . . . if you're really going to understand how it works: "If you think you can run a business from your office, you're crazy!" I know I heard that lecture more than once, and I can recall that it often ended with the caution, "Never forget how to get your hands dirty." (20)

13. Roberts and Vickers, *Distant Force*, 30, 65.

14. Source of both quotes is Roberts and Vickers, *Distant Force*, 200.

15. Joseph Fuller and Michael Jensen, "Just Say No to Wall Street: Putting a Stop to the Earnings Game," *Journal of Applied Corporate Finance* 22, no. 1 (Winter 2010); *Harvard Business School NOM Unit Working Paper No. 10–090*. Available at SSRN: http://ssrn.com/abstract=1583563.

16. Train, *The Money Masters*, 24.

17. Roberts and Vickers, *Distant Force*, 65–66, and James Nisbet, *The Entrepreneur* (Charlotte, NC: Capital Technology, 1976), 148–49. Thanks to Professor Tom O'Brien for referring me to this source.

18. For example: "Global Mergers and Acquisitions Reached a Record High in the First Quarter," *CNBC*, March 30, 2018, https://www.cnbc .com/2018/03/30/global-ma-in-the-first-quarter-of-2018.html.

19. Referring to the earnings yield, which is the reciprocal of the P/E ratio (1/15 = 6.67 percent).

20. Roberts and Vickers, *Distant Force*, 103, 104.

21. A. F. Ehrbar, "Henry Singleton's Mystifying $400-Million Flyer," *Fortune*, January 16, 1978: 66. Copy courtesy of Leon G. Cooperman.

22. Jason Zweig, "Defining the New Profession," in *Benjamin Graham: Building a Profession* (New York: McGraw-Hill, 2010), 43. Note also the buyback analysis in S. L. Mintz, "Working on the Railroad," *Institutional Investor* (May 2016), 27.

23. Roberts and Vickers, *Distant Force*, 121, 288. Calculations are mine and have been rounded.

24. Roberts and Vickers, *Distant Force*, 121, 288.

25. Robert Flaherty, "The Singular Henry Singleton," *Forbes*, July 9, 1979, 46.

26. Roberts and Vickers, *Distant Force*, 121, 288. Calculations are mine and have been rounded.

27. Leon G. Cooperman conversation with the author on June 5, 2010.

28. Nisbet, *The Entrepreneur*, 164, which originally listed the book as "The World History of Interest Rates," which I could not find. The actual book was likely the first edition of the late Sidney Homer's seminal *A History of Interest Rates*, which is now in its fourth edition: Sidney Homer and Richard Sylla, *A History of Interest Rates*, 4th ed. (Hoboken, NJ: Wiley, 2005 [1963]).

29. Roberts and Vickers, *Distant Force*, 229.

30. Eric Savitz, "Son of Teledyne: The Conglomerate Spins Off Its Insurance Operations," *Barron's*, April 23, 1990, 16.

31. Roberts and Vickers, *Distant Force*, 278.

32. Leon G. Cooperman conversation with the author on June 5, 2010.

33. Leon G. Cooperman, *A Case Study in Financial Brilliance: Teledyne, Inc., Dr. Henry E. Singleton*, November 28, 2007, 5.

34. Simon Ramo, "Eulogy Delivered on September 8, 1999: Remembering Henry Singleton," in Roberts and Vickers, *Distant Force*, 281. According to Cooperman, Singleton felt it was logical to court the press when a corporate manager was using his stock to fund growth. Other than that, he felt corporate managers should focus on managing their businesses. "Don't complain,

don't explain" is how Cooperman summed it up to me in our June 5, 2010, conversation.

35. Joseph Badaracco, *Leading Quietly: An Unorthodox Guide to Doing the Right Things* (Boston, MA: Harvard Business School Press, 2002), 34.

36. Roberts and Vickers, *Distant Force*, 125.

37. James Hagerty, *The Fateful History of Fannie Mae: New Deal Birth to Mortgage Crisis Fall* (Charleston, SC: History, 2012).

38. Singleton is briefly profiled in Anthony J. Mayo and Nitin Nohria, *In Their Time: The Greatest Business Leaders of the Twentieth Century* (Boston, MA: Harvard Business School Press Press, 2005), and in William Thorndike, *The Outsiders: Eight Unconventional CEOs and Their Radically Rational Blueprint for Success* (Boston, MA: Harvard Business School Press, 2012).

39. Flaherty, "The Singular Henry Singleton," 45. For information on Royal Little, see Robert Sobel, chapter 2 in *The Rise and Fall of the Conglomerate Kings* (New York: Stein and Day, 1984).

40. Grant, *Mr. Market Miscalculates*, xxi.

41. Conversation with the author on June 2, 2010.

42. Copy courtesy of Lee Cooperman.

Appendix 5.1. Evaluating a Stock Buyback

This appendix contains material from *Strategy & Leadership*, © 2010 by Emerald Publishing, which is reprinted with permission. The author would like to thank Leon G. Cooperman for helpful questions, comments, and suggestions on earlier drafts of this appendix. Any error or omission is solely my fault.

1. Benjamin Graham, David Dodd, and Sidney Cottle, *Security Analysis*, 4th ed. (New York: McGraw-Hill, 1962), 521.

2. Robert Hagstrom, *The Warren Buffet Way*, 3rd ed. (Hoboken, NJ: Wiley, 2014), 106. As Maggie Mahar observed, "Responsible management buys back its company's stock only when it is a bargain." Mahar, *Bull!—A History of the Boom, 1982–1999* (New York: Harper, 2003), 133.

3. Leon G. Cooperman, *Stock Repurchase: Value Creative or Value Destructive?*, November 28, 2007, 33–36. For information on the late Larry Tisch see Christopher Winans, *The King of Cash: The Inside Story of Laurence Tisch* (New York: Wiley, 1995).

4. Mark Robichaux, *Cable Cowboy: John Malone and the Rise of the Modern Cable Business* (Hoboken, NJ: Wiley, 2002), 273. Note also Christopher Marangi, *Financial Engineering Playbook*, Gabelli Funds, January 2014.

5. L. J. Rittenhouse, *Investing Between the Lines: How to Make Smarter Decisions by Decoding CEO Communications* (New York: McGraw-Hill, 2013), 156–57.

6. James Grant, *Grant's Interest Rate Observer*, March 7, 2014, 1. See also the following observation of Professor John Graham: "It does not appear that companies are successfully timing repurchases of their stock in years when it is cheap and undervalued." S. L. Mintz, "Buybacks Under Scrutiny," *Institutional Investor*, September 2014, 122. See also Mintz, "Working on the Railroad." By way of background, Mintz is the coauthor of value investor John Neff's autobiography, *John Neff on Investing* (New York: Wiley, 1999).

7. "A great mystery of the corporate world is the tendency of management to buy high and sell low." Edward Chancellor, *Capital Returns: Investing Through the Capital Cycle, A Money Manager's Reports, 2002–2015* (London, UK: Palgrave, 2016), 80.

8. For more information see, for example, Edward Chancellor, ed., *Capital Account: A Money Manager's Reports on a Turbulent Decade 1993–2002* (New York: Palgrave, 2016).

9. An article in *The Economist* was critical of share buybacks and suggested that it was not possible for firms to buy back their shares at a discount, and that if it was possible to do so, such purchases would somehow mistreat the shareholders who sold out. For more information see "Share Buy-backs: The Repurchase Revolution," *The Economist*, September 13, 2014, 72. First, while it is true that many corporate managers overpay for financial assets—including their own stock—it is most definitely *not* true that all corporate managers overpay for financial assets, as the cases of Berkshire Hathaway, Loews, Liberty Media, etc., illustrate. Second, so long as no one forces investors to sell their shares, no outside party, and that includes *The Economist*, has any standing to criticize voluntary transactions. Investors sell their shares for any number of reasons (value being subjective, to say nothing of cash needs at the moment of sale), and thus it would be inappropriate to prevent them from doing so, including when a corporate manager, or business magazine, may feel that the shares they are selling are undervalued.

10. Cooperman, *Stock Repurchase*, 23.

Appendix 5.2. Managing Funding Obligations

1. Benjamin Graham and David Dodd, *Security Analysis*, 6th ed. (New York: McGraw-Hill, 2009), 594.

2. James Grant, *Minding Mr. Market: Ten Years on Wall Street with Grant's Interest Rate Observer* (New York: Farrar, Straus and Giroux, 1993), 298.

3. Martin J. Whitman and Fernando Diz noted that "Franco Modigliani and Merton Miller, two eminent economists, received a Nobel Prize for postulating, 'Assuming that managements work in the best interests of stockholders, corporate capitalizations are a matter of indifference.' What utter nonsense!" *Distress Investing: Principles and Technique* (Hoboken, NJ: Wiley, 2009), xvii.

4. Michael Lewis, *The Big Short: Inside The Doomsday Machine* (New York: Norton, 2010), 174.

5. *Robert Merton: Lessons from Crashing the Financial System*, CFA Institute Conference, October 7, 2012, YouTube, https://www.youtube.com /watch?v=lFP9DE0Wjyc. Thanks to value investor Mitch Julis for referring me to this video clip.

6. Maury Klein, *The Power Makers: Steam, Electricity, and the Men Who Invested Modern America* (New York: Bloomsbury, 2008), 292–96.

7. Klein, chapter 18 in *The Power Makers*. According to Mr. Westinghouse's public statement at the time: "When the Pittsburgh Clearing House Committee . . . concluded that, although the Westinghouse Electric and Manufacturing Company and the Westinghouse Machine Company were solvent, receiverships were advisable as the best means of protecting all concerned, it was clearly our duty to follow their friendly advice. The necessity of the receiverships is due solely to the financial stringency and the consequent inability to renew our maturing paper." William Silber, *When Washington Shut Down Wall Street: The Great Financial Crisis of 1914 and the Origins of America's Monetary Supremacy* (Princeton, NJ: Princeton, 2007), 52.

8. Klein, *The Power Makers*, 394.

9. "It doesn't matter whether a company is big or small. Capital structure matters. It always has and always will." Michael Milken, "Why Capital Structure Matters," *Wall Street Journal* (April 21, 2009), http://online.wsj .com/news/articles/SB124027187331937083.

10. "Unlike the conventional academic view, we are of the opinion that capital structure arises out of a process that involves meeting the needs and desires of a multiplicity of constituencies, including various creditors, regulators, rating agencies, managements and other control groups, OPMIs [outside passive minority investors], and the company itself." Whitman and Diz, *Distress Investing*, 38.

6. Managerial "Rationality"

This chapter contains material from the *Journal of Investing*, © 2017 by Institutional Investor, which is reprinted with permission. The author would like to thank Brian Bruce, Larry Pitkowski, and Robert Hagstrom for helpful questions, comments, and suggestions on earlier drafts of this chapter. Any errors or omissions are solely my fault.

1. Benjamin Graham and David Dodd, *Security Analysis*, 6th ed. (New York: McGraw-Hill, 2009), 68.

2. As quoted by Irving Kahn and Robert Milne, *Benjamin Graham: The Father of Financial Analysis* (Charlottesville, VA: Financial Analysts Research Foundation, 1977), 48.

3. Copy courtesy of Leon G. Cooperman.

4. Carl Hovey, *The Life Story of J. Pierpont Morgan: A Biography* (New York: Sturgis & Walton, 1911), 98–99.

5. As Hovey, *The Life Story of J. Pierpont Morgan*, explained, "There was no logic in [the railroad] business. It was not business; it was a dogfight. The conservative journals of the day, unable to find the word for it, coined a phrase—they called it Criminal Competition" (125). This is obviously an interesting choice of words, even from a historical perspective; nevertheless, and as James Grant has observed, "Markets, after all, are only as rational as we are." Maggie Mahar, *Bull!—A History of the Boom, 1982–1999* (New York: Harper, 2003), 69. See Alfred J. Chandler, *The Visible Hand: The Managerial Revolution in American Business* (Cambridge, MA: Belknap, 1977), for a superb historical analysis of the railroad industry.

6. Willy Shih, *Rational Choice and Managerial Decision Making*, HBS case services #9-614-048 (January 14, 2014), 1–2.

7. Robert Hagstrom, *Investing: The Last Liberal Art*, 2nd ed. (New York: Columbia, 2013), 151. Hagstrom and value investor Larry Pitkowsky inspired the research that resulted in this chapter.

8. Keith Stanovich, *What Intelligence Tests Miss: The Psychology of Rational Thought* (New Haven, CT: Yale, 2009), 16. On this definition see also Robert Hagstrom, *The Warren Buffett Way*, 3rd ed. (Hoboken, NJ: Wiley, 2014), 205–206, and Michael Mauboussin and Dan Callahan, *IQ versus EQ: Differentiating Smarts from Decision-Making Skills*," Credit Suisse white paper, May 12, 2015, https://www.valuewalk.com/wp-content/uploads/2015/05/document-1048541371.pdf. By way of background, Keith E. Stanovich is Professor Emeritus of Applied Psychology and Human Development at the University of Toronto. See his website at http://www

.keithstanovich.com/Site/Home.html. Professor Stanovich's work raises obvious behavioral economic implications. For example, Daniel Kahneman, *Thinking, Fast and Slow* (New York: Farrar, Strauss and Giroux, 2011), observed, "Time will tell whether the distinction between intelligence and rationality can lead to new discoveries" (49).

9. Joseph Calandro, Jr., "Turnaround Value and Valuation: Reassessing Scott Paper," *Journal of Private Equity* (Winter 2011): 67–78.

10. The video can be found at http://www.c-span.org/video/?76876-1 /corporate-responsibilities.

11. This supposition was confirmed during a 2015 conversation the author had with someone involved in the hiring of Dunlap at Sunbeam, who shall remain nameless.

12. "Chainsaw Al: He Anointed Himself America's Best CEO. But Al Dunlap Drove Sunbeam into the Ground," *Businessweek*, October 17, 1999, https://www.bloomberg.com/news/articles/1999-10-17/chainsaw-al.

13. Per Benjamin Graham, *The Intelligent Investor*, 4th ed. (New York: Harper & Row, 1973), "the concept of risk" pertains "solely to a loss of value which either is realized through actual sale, or is caused by a significant deterioration in the company's position—or, more frequently perhaps, is the result of the payment of an excessive price in relation to the intrinsic worth of the security" (61).

14. Benjamin Graham and David Dodd, *Security Analysis*, 6th ed. (New York: McGraw-Hill, 2009), 582. The reason for this can be found in market behavior itself. As Benjamin Graham observed, "Most of the time common stocks are subject to irrational and excessive price fluctuations in both directions, as the consequence of the ingrained tendency of most people to speculate or gamble—*i.e., to give way to hope, fear and greed.*" Kahn and Milne, *Benjamin Graham*, 48; italics original.

15. Seth A. Klarman, *Margin of Safety: Risk-Adverse Value Investing Strategies for the Thoughtful Investor* (New York: HarperBusiness, 1991), observed that corporate managers "not only respond to uncertainty; they sometimes enhance it by taking unpredictable or ill-considered actions" (146), which certainly seems to have been the case here.

16. Joseph Calandro, Jr., "A Leader's Guide to Strategic Risk Management," *Strategy & Leadership* 43 (2015): 32.

17. "Chainsaw Al," *Businessweek*.

18. Eric Savitz, "Son of Teledyne: The Conglomerate Spins Off Its Insurance Operations," *Barron's*, April 23, 1990, 16.

19. This is a basic but important point. As investor Stanley Druckenmiller has observed, "Frankly, even today, many analysts still do not know what makes their particular stocks go up and down." Jack Schwager, *The New*

Market Wizards: Conversations with America's Top Traders (Glenelg, MD: Marketplace, 2008), 222. Such concerns obviously matter less in liquidations and certain (e.g., non-turnaround-related) distressed investments.

20. The deal did not close but the potential buyer was comfortable walking away for risk management reasons.

21. L. J. Rittenhouse, "2015 Rittenhouse Rankings: CEO Candor & Culture Survey," *Rittenhouse Rankings* (2015), http://www.rittenhouserankings .com/wp-content/uploads/2016/12/2015-Rittenhouse-Rankings-Candor -AnalyticsTM-Survey-Report.pdf. For background, see L. J. Rittenhouse, *Investing Between the Lines: How to Make Smarter Decisions by Decoding CEO Communications* (New York: McGraw-Hill, 2013). Interestingly, in Robert Havers's profile of the leadership characteristics of George C. Marshall, the late General of the Army, Secretary of State, and Nobel Peace Prize winner, candor was listed as the first leadership characteristic. Havers, "The Servant Leader in the 21st Century," *Capitol Ideas*, July– August 2015, http://www.csg.org/pubs/capitolideas/2015_july_aug/servant _leader.aspx.

22. William E. Fruhan, Jr., "Corporate Raiders: Head'em Off at Value Gap," *Harvard Business Review*, July–August 1988: 63–69.

23. For more information see " 'It Is the Judgment That Counts'—Michael Price," *Graham & Doddsville* 12 (Spring 2011): 1, 4, and Bruce Greenwald, et al., *Value Investing: From Graham to Buffett and Beyond* (Hoboken, NJ: Wiley, 2001), 246. Note also Seth A. Klarman, "Preface to the Sixth Edition: The Timeless Wisdom of Graham and Dodd," in Graham and Dodd (2009), xxxv–xxxvi.

24. James Grant, "Anticipating Mr. Friedman," *Grant's Interest Rate Observer* 33, no. 24 (December 11, 2015): 8.

25. Grant, "Anticipating Mr. Friedman," 9.

26. Warren Buffett, preface to Benjamin Graham, *The Intelligent Investor*, 4th ed. (New York: Harper & Row, 1973), vii.

7. Corporate Management and "Modern Security Analysis"

This chapter contains material from *Strategy & Leadership*, © 2014 by Emerald Publishing, which is reprinted with permission. The author would like to thank the late Martin J. Whitman and Fernando Diz for helpful questions, comments, and suggestions on earlier drafts of this chapter. Any errors or omissions are solely my fault.

1. Martin J. Whitman and Martin Shubik, *The Aggressive Conservative Investor* (Hoboken, NJ, Wiley, 2006 [1979]), 338.

2. Martin J. Whitman and Fernando Diz, *Modern Security Analysis: Understanding Wall Street Fundamentals* (Hoboken, NJ: Wiley, 2013), 467.

3. Mr. Whitman's career includes a highly successful distressed investment that was generated by the failure of the Penn Central Railroad in the early 1970s (for information see: http://www.thirdave.com/who-we-are/history/). For information on the historic failure of the Penn Central, see Robert Sobel, *The Fallen Colossus: The Great Crash of the Penn Central* (Washington, DC: Beard, 2000).

4. Steve Denning, "The Financial Times Slams 'The World's Dumbest Idea,'" *Forbes*, September 2, 2014, http://www.forbes.com/sites/stevedenning /2014/09/02/the-financial-times-slams-the-worlds-dumbest-idea/.

5. Whitman and Diz, *Modern Security Analysis*, 104.

6. Whitman and Diz, *Modern Security Analysis*, 105.

7. As Whitman and Diz observed, "Compared with value investors, great economists from Keynes to Modigliani and Miller [who invented the capital structure irrelevance proposition] seem largely oblivious to the very important role creditworthiness plays in any industrial economy" (202). For a profile of modern financial economics see Peter Bernstein, *Capital Ideas: The Improbable Origins of Modern Wall Street* (New York: Free Press, 1992), and Peter Bernstein, *Capital Ideas Evolving* (Hoboken, NJ: Wiley, 2007).

8. Michael Lewis, *The Big Short: Inside The Doomsday Machine* (New York: Norton, 2010), 174.

9. There is a difference between value, as defined by the price of equity, and wealth. As used here, "Wealth creation is a result not only of successful operations but also judicious investing and having attractive access to capital markets." Martin J. Whitman, "Letter from the Chairman," *Third Avenue Funds: Portfolio Manager Commentary*, July 31, 2014, 1. See Whitman and Diz, *Modern Security Analysis*, 20–21 for more information.

10. Rodney Boyd, *Fatal Risk* (Hoboken, NJ: Wiley, 2011), 206–208.

11. Whitman and Diz, *Modern Security Analysis*, 96.

12. L. J. Rittenhouse, *Investing Between the Lines: How to Make Smarter Decisions by Decoding CEO Communications* (New York: McGraw-Hill, 2013), 75. See also Martin Mayer, *The Fed: The Inside Story of How the World's Most Powerful Financial Institution Drives the Markets* (New York: Free Press, 2001), 20. Thanks to Fernando Diz for pointing out a correction.

13. Seth A. Klarman, *Margin of Safety: Risk-Adverse Value Investing Strategies for the Thoughtful Investor* (New York: HarperBusiness, 1991), 69.

14. Ron Chernow, *The House of Morgan: An American Banking Dynasty and the Rise of Modern Finance* (New York: Atlantic, 1990), 154.

15. For more information see Joseph Calandro, Jr., *Value Investing General Principles*, September 21, 2016, available at SSRN: https://ssrn.com/abstract=2575429.

16. Paul Carroll and Chunka Mui, *Billion Dollar Lessons: What You Can Learn from the Most Inexcusable Business Failures of the Last 25 Years* (New York: Portfolio, 2008), and Joseph Calandro, Jr., "Learning from the Expensive Failures of Others," *Strategy & Leadership* 37, no. 5 (2009): 47–49.

17. Carroll and Mui, *Billion Dollar Lessons*, 26.

18. Michiyo Nakamoto and David Wighton, "Citigroup Chief Stays Bullish on Buy-Outs," *Financial Times*, July 9, 2007, http://www.ft.com/cms/s/0/80e2987a-2e50-11dc-821c-0000779fd2ac.html#axzz3Cemk6vSD.

19. "Misfortune has a way of choosing some unprecedented means or other of impressing its power on those who might be said to have forgotten it." Robin Alexander Campbell, tr., Seneca, *Letters from a Stoic* (New York: Penguin Classics, 2014), 206.

20. Whitman and Diz (2013), 32. In both corporate management and security analysis today, "the main item of underused information is the balance sheet." Martin J. Whitman, "A Fresh Look at the Efficient Market Hypothesis," in Philip Jenks and Stephen Eckett, ed., *The Global Investor Book of Investing Rules: Invaluable Advice from 150 Master Investors* (New York: Financial Times, 2002), 471.

21. One of the most dramatic examples of this is the Enron case as profiled by David F. Hawkins and Jacob Cohen, *Enron Corporation: May 6, 2001 Sell Recommendation*, HBS case services #9-104-075 (March 7, 2006). The analysis profiled in this case has been attributed to famed short-seller James Chanos.

22. Whitman and Diz, *Modern Security Analysis*, 169.

23. For detailed examples of changes of control through the acquisition of distressed credits, see Martin J. Whitman and Fernando Diz, *Distress Investing: Principles and Techniques* (Hoboken, NJ: Wiley, 2009).

24. Whitman and Diz, *Modern Security Analysis*, 357.

25. Whitman and Diz, *Modern Security Analysis*, 405.

26. Whitman and Diz, *Modern Security Analysis*, 432.

27. Whitman and Diz, *Modern Security Analysis*, 467.

28. Other markets can be very efficient such as those for eminently creditworthy debt securities (e.g., U.S. Treasuries) and those for securities based on a small number of computer programmable variables (such as options). This is a rather narrow, and self-liquidating, section of the overall market. However, even these markets can be subject to severe occasional disruption. For more information see Nassim Nicholas Taleb, *The Black Swan: The Impact of the Highly Improbable* (New York: Random House, 2007).

29. For more information see Michael Lewis, "New New Money," in *Panic: The Story of Modern Financial Insanity* (New York: Norton, 2009), 176–85.

30. George Goodman aka Adam Smith referred to this phenomenon as "supermoney" in his book of the same name, *Supermoney* (New York: Random House, 1972). He described it by way of the hypothetical example of Pediatricians, Inc., a small firm that just went public: "Their old net worth—the sum of stethoscopes, fluoroscopes and lollipops—came, let us say, to $10,000. Their new net worth is $1,500,000. The difference of $1,490,000 is new money to the economy, just as if the Fed had printed it, and should be included in all the calculations of the money supply" (20–21). Modern central bankers and academic economists refer to this phenomenon as the "wealth effect," which they do not include in their calculations of the money supply.

31. "If there is one lesson to be learned from the mix of bargains and dross on Alibaba's e-commerce sites, it is 'buyer beware.' Its shares and those of similarly structured companies may reinforce that idea." For more information see "Out of Control," *The Economist*, September 20, 2014, 67.

32. "Fundamental finance covers the following areas: Value investing, Distress investing, Control investing, Credit analysis, First and second stage venture capital investing." Whitman and Diz, *Modern Security Analysis*, 5.

33. Whitman and Diz, chapter 25 in *Modern Security Analysis*.

34. Whitman and Diz, *Modern Security Analysis*, p. 120.

35. For more information see Whitman and Diz, chapter 8 in *Modern Security Analysis*.

36. Whitman and Diz, *Modern Security Analysis*, 127.

37. Whitman and Diz, *Modern Security Analysis*, 120–21.

38. Whitman and Diz, *Modern Security Analysis*, 162–63.

39. Whitman and Diz, chapter 26 in *Modern Security Analysis*.

40. Whitman and Diz, *Modern Security Analysis*, 432.

41. Mark Robichaux, *Cable Cowboy: John Malone and the Rise of the Modern Cable Business* (Hoboken, NJ: Wiley, 2002), 239.

42. Robichaux, *Cable Cowboy*, 245–46.

8. Value Realization Is "The Most Important Thing"

This chapter contains material from the *Journal of Private Equity*, © 2012 by Institutional Investor, which is reprinted with permission. The author would like to thank Howard Marks for helpful questions, comments, and suggestions on earlier drafts of this chapter. Any error or omission is solely my fault.

1. Rodney Klein, ed., *Benjamin Graham on Value Investing: Enduring Lessons from the Father of Value Investing* (New York: McGraw-Hill, 2009), 199.

2. Howard Marks, *The Most Important Thing: Uncommon Sense for the Thoughtful Investor* (New York: Columbia, 2011), 20.

3. Most investors would prefer relatively quick decisions and activities so tension between the short term and long term can develop. As a professional value investor, Marks (2011) focuses on longer-term performance (171).

4. See also Howard Marks, "Unshackling Bonds," in Benjamin Graham and David Dodd, *Security Analysis*, 6th ed. (New York: McGraw-Hill, 2009), 123–40.

5. Marks's presentation took place on April 5, 2012.

6. For more information see Walter Kiechel, *The Lords of Strategy: The Secret Intellectual History of the New Corporate World* (Boston, MA: Harvard Business School Press, 2010).

7. Marks, *The Most Important Thing*, 3. I changed the word in brackets from "investors" to "competitors" but left in the reference to "investment" later in the passage because strategy inherently pertains to investment. For more information see Pankaj Ghemawat, *Commitment: The Dynamic of Strategy* (New York: Free Press, 1991).

8. Marks, *The Most Important Thing*, 14.

9. Marks, *The Most Important Thing*, 11.

10. Marks, *The Most Important Thing*, 93–94.

11. Marks, *The Most Important Thing*, 25.

12. Marks, *The Most Important Thing*, 95.

13. Marks, *The Most Important Thing*, 111.

14. Marks, *The Most Important Thing*, 149.

15. Robert S. Kaplan and David P. Norton, *The Strategy-focused Organization: How Balanced Scorecard Companies Thrive in the New Business Environment* (Boston, MA: Harvard Business School Press, 2001), 17.

16. Robert Slater, *Jack Welch and the GE Way* (New York: McGraw-Hill, 1999), 165.

17. *Berkshire Hathaway Annual Report, 1996*, http://www.berkshirehathaway.com/1996ar/1996.html.

18. Marks, *The Most Important Thing*, 151. I changed the word in brackets from "investor" to "competitor."

19. Diane Vaughan, *The Challenger Launch Decision: Risky Technology, Culture, and Deviance at NASA* (Chicago, IL: Chicago, 1997 [1996]).

20. Marks, *The Most Important Thing*, 121. Warren Buffett observed, "For some unexplained reason, [many] investors are so infatuated with the notion of what tomorrow may bring that they ignore today's business

reality." Robert Hagstrom, *The Warren Buffett Way* (New York: Wiley, 1994), 78.

21. Marks, *The Most Important Thing*, 143.

22. Marks, *The Most Important Thing*, 36, 39, 176.

23. Marks, *The Most Important Thing*, 33. As Benjamin Graham and David Dodd observed, "attempts to increase yield at the expense of safety are likely to be unprofitable." *Security Analysis*, 6th ed. (New York: McGraw-Hill, 2009), 161.

24. Benjamin Graham, *The Intelligent Investor*, 4th ed. (New York: Harper & Row, 1973), 281. Graham earlier observed that "the margin guarantees only that [an investment] has a better chance for profit than for loss—not that loss is impossible." Benjamin Graham, *The Intelligent Investor* (New York: Harper & Row, 1949), 245.

25. Marks, *The Most Important Thing*, 26; italics original.

26. Marks, *The Most Important Thing*, 76. There are, of course, significant behavioral ramifications to each of these stages. For example, with respect to the third stage, it has been said, "No bull stock market is complete before the debut of the kind of equity that's valued on *the quality of its narrative*. It's anticipation of earnings, not their actual arrival, that sets the speculative heart fluttering in the late stages of a proper levitation." James Grant, *Grant's Interest Rate Observer* 31, no. 22 (November 15, 2013): 1. In the same issue Grant went on to quote the following: "What a promoter needed to launch a new stock, apart from a persuasive tongue and a resourceful accountant, was to have a 'story'—an easily grasped concept, preferably related to some current national fad or preoccupation, that *sounded* as if it would lead to profits" (italics original). This quote is from John Brooks, *The Go-Go Years: The Drama and Crashing Finale of Wall Street's Bullish 60s* (New York: Allworth, 1998), 270.

27. Marks, *The Most Important Thing*, 77. This model rationalizes to the eight-stage business model presented in chapter 5 of my earlier book, *Applied Value Investing* (New York: McGraw-Hill, 2009).

28. Marks, *The Most Important Thing*, 77–78.

9. Value Realization at GEICO

This chapter contains material from the *Journal of Private Equity*, © 2011 by Institutional Investor, which is reprinted with permission. The author would like to thank James E. Schrager for helpful questions, comments, and suggestions on earlier drafts of this chapter. Any errors or omissions are solely my fault.

1. Benjamin Graham, *The Memoirs of the Dean of Wall Street* (New York: McGraw-Hill, 1996), 332.

2. Warren Buffett and Carol Loomis, "Mr. Buffett on the Stock Market," *Fortune*, November 22, 1999, http://money.cnn.com/magazines/fortune /fortune_archive/1999/11/22/269071/.

3. For an example see Bruce Henderson, *Henderson on Corporate Strategy* (Cambridge, MA: Abt Books, 1979).

4. "The conglomerates realized disappointing earnings growth and risk reduction during the 1970s, and this disappointment was followed, in the late 1970s and through the 1980s, by a wave of takeovers, divestitures, and management replacement." Robert S. Kaplan and David P. Norton, *Alignment: Using the Balanced Scorecard to Create Corporate Synergies* (Boston, MA: Harvard Business School Press, 2006), 45.

5. Wikipedia, http://en.wikipedia.org/wiki/Leo_Goodwin,_Sr.

6. *Berkshire Hathaway Annual Report, 2004*, http://www.berkshireha-thaway.com/letters/2004ltr.pdf.

7. See Joseph Calandro, Jr., and Thomas O'Brien, "A User-Friendly Introduction to Property-Casualty Claim Reserves," *Risk Management and Insurance Review* 7, no. 2 (2004): 177–187 for information on insurance reserving.

8. Thanks to Bob Glasspiegel for bringing this to my attention. Interestingly, GEICO's underwriting-related issues were likely exacerbated by inflation (e.g., higher gasoline costs), which served to generate both regulatory and competitive rate reductions.

9. Byrne passed away on March 7, 2013. For more information see, for example, Douglas Martin, "John J. Byrne Dies at 80; Turned Around Geico," *New York Times*, March 12, 2013, http://www.nytimes.com/2013/03/13 /business/john-j-byrne-dies-at-80-saved-geico-from-bankruptcy.html?_r=0.

10. *Berkshire Hathaway Annual Report, 2004*. This is not to say that Byrne never undertook unsatisfactory initiatives. For example, he was involved in diversifying GEICO into reinsurance via the firm's 1981 Resolute Group initiative. Thanks to Bob Glasspiegel for bringing this to my attention.

11. The original source for the article is http://www.designs.valueinvestor insight.com/bonus/bonuscontent/docs/The_Security_I_Like_Best_Buffett _1951.pdf but it no longer seems to be posted.

12. "GEICO, one of the great postwar growth stocks, had plunged into scandal and loss, with a stock price to match. From a high of 42 a share in 1974, it found its way down to 4 7/8 before Buffett and Jack Byrne mounted their now-famous 11th-hour rescue in 1976. Even then, it was sawed in half; Buffett paid 2 1/8 for 500,000 shares in the month of the U.S. bicentennial."

James Grant, *Mr. Market Miscalculates: The Bubble Years and Beyond* (Mt. Jackson, VA: Axios, 2008), 387.

13. *Berkshire Hathaway Annual Report, 2009*; http://www.berkshire hathaway.com/letters/2009ltr.pdf.

14. Joseph Calandro, Jr. and Scott Lane, "A New Competitive Analysis Tool: The Relative Profitability and Growth Matrix," *Strategy & Leadership* 35, no. 2 (2007): 30–38.

15. William E. Fruhan, Jr., *Financial Strategy: Studies in the Creation, Transfer, and Destruction of Shareholder Value* (Homewood, IL: Irwin, 1979).

16. According to Benjamin Graham, David Dodd, and Sidney Cottle, *Security Analysis*, 4th ed. (New York: McGraw-Hill, 1962): "An outstanding company increases its profit more rapidly than the rest of the industry. . . . Failure to expand as fast as the industry as a whole is generally considered an unsatisfactory element in the picture and a sign of weakness in the company's position or management" (671).

17. We use ROE (based on average book equity) and premium (or sales) growth as they are commonly used measures. In practice, any profitability and growth measure could be used to construct an RPG matrix, but it must be remembered that the purpose of the matrix is to help screen for opportunities that will be subjected to valuation. Investment decisions should obviously *not* be made on the basis of matrix analysis alone. For more information on matrix analyses in general see Alex Lowy and Phil Hood, *The Power of the 2x2 Matrix* (San Francisco, CA: Jossey-Bass, 2004).

18. Premium "earned" is that portion of premium written that has been earned over the past year; for example, a policy sold on January 1 of a given year would be fully earned at the end of the year compared to a policy sold on December 1, which would be one-twelfth earned. "Net" premium is gross premium less ceded premium where "ceded" means transferred to a reinsurer(s).

19. We compare GEICO's ROE with the insurance industry's return on surplus, "policyholders' surplus" being the insurance version of shareholders' equity. Surplus is typically derived more conservatively than equity; however, as the insurance industry is composed of many public, private, and mutual organizations, a case could be made that its surplus is relatively equal to equity over time. That said, the choice of which measure to use is left to the analyst; in this case, comparing GEICO's return on surplus with the industry's results in a much higher degree of relative profitability—per the author's calculations—and as such the more conservative approach was used here.

20. This is supposition on my part as I am not privy to GEICO's internal and presumably confidential strategic materials, but if it is correct, it was a

wise strategic move. According to Michael Porter, *Competitive Advantage: Creating and Sustaining Superior Performance* (New York: Free Press, 1998 [1985]), "a leader making extraordinary profits may provide an umbrella for a challenger, if high profits more than offset the costs of attack" (535).

21. Porter, *Competitive Advantage*, 3.

22. Porter, *Competitive Advantage*, 17.

23. Krishna Palepu, Paul Healy, and Victor Bernard, chapter 10 in *Business Analysis & Valuation: Using Financial Statements*, 2nd ed. (Cincinnati, OH: South-Western Publishing, 2000), and Pankaj Ghemawat, *Sustaining Superior Performance: Commitments and Capabilities*, HBS Case Services #9-798-008, July 31, 1997. Benjamin Graham understood the transitory nature of performance as he and David Dodd opened *Security Analysis* with Horace's famous quote: "Many shall be restored that now are fallen and many shall fall that are now in honor." However, "it does not say when." Seth A. Klarman, "Why Value Investors Are Different," *Barron's*, February 15, 1999, 39.

24. *Berkshire Hathaway Annual Report, 2000*, http://www.berkshire hathaway.com/2000ar/2000letter.html.

25. The actual calculations (in thousands) are growth value of $3,588,388 = [(earnings of $257,465 / net asset value of $1,486,858) / required return of 11.2 percent] * earnings power value of $2,323,684, which when divided by the amount of shares comes to $106.5 as shown in the exhibit. Calandro, *Applied Value Investing* (New York: McGraw-Hill), 56.

26. Stan Hinden, "The GEICO Deal: How Billionaire Buffett Bid at $70," *The Washington Post*, November 6, 1995, http://proquest.umi.com/pqdweb ?did=19440424&Fmt=3&clientId=61593&RQT=309&VName=PQT.

27. For more information on this approach see Bruce Greenwald, et al., *Value Investing—From Graham to Buffett & Beyond* (New York: Wiley, 2001), 133–37. From Benjamin Graham and David Dodd, *Security Analysis*, 3rd ed.: "Obviously, if [an acquirer] can get the future for *nothing*, i.e., if the price reflects only the past record, he is making a sound investment." (New York: McGraw-Hill, 1951 [1934]): 399, italics original.

28. For more information see Porter, *Competitive Advantage*.

29. There are obviously much more rigorous insurance value chains that could be presented here, but the profile offered is sufficient for our purposes in this chapter.

30. For more information on the Balanced Scorecard see Robert S. Kaplan and David P. Norton, *The Balanced Scorecard* (Boston, MA: Harvard Business School Press, 1996). Other categories could be used in lieu of these four. For more information see, for example, Andy Neely, et al., *The Performance Prism: The Scorecard for Measuring and Managing Business Success* (London: FT Prentice Hall, 2002).

31. Strategically integrating scale with cost and differentiation follows the work of the late corporate strategy theorist Joe S. Bain, *Barriers to New Competition: Their Character and Consequences in Manufacturing Industries* (Cambridge, MA: Harvard, 1956).

32. For more information see Joseph Calandro, Jr., and Scott Lane, "The Insurance Performance Measure: Bringing Value to the Insurance Industry," *Journal of Applied Corporate Finance* 14, no. 4 (2002): 94–99.

33. See, for example, the *Berkshire Hathaway Annual Report, 1999,* http://www.berkshirehathaway.com/letters/1999htm.html.

34. Porter, *Competitive Advantage.*

35. *Berkshire Hathaway Annual Report, 1996,* http://www.berkshire hathaway.com/letters/1996.html. Note that the criteria of profitability and growth reconcile with RPG matrix variables.

36. *Berkshire Hathaway Annual Report, 1996.*

37. W. Bruce Chew, "No-Nonsense Guide to Measuring Productivity," *Harvard Business Review*, January–February 1988: 3–9.

38. Answers, http://www.answers.com/topic/experience-curve-effects. Note also Alan Schmidt and Samuel Wood, *The Growth of Intel and the Learning Curve*, Stanford Case Services #S-OIT-27 (June 1999).

39. *Berkshire Hathaway Annual Report, 2006,* http://www.berkshire hathaway.com/letters/2006ltr.pdf.

40. *Berkshire Hathaway Annual Report, 2008,* http://www.berkshire hathaway.com/letters/2008ltr.pdf.

41. Berkshire Hathaway annual reports; calculations are mine and have been rounded.

42. *Berkshire Hathaway Annual Report, 2007,* http://www.berkshire hathaway.com/letters/2007ltr.pdf.

43. *Berkshire Hathaway Annual Report, 2009,* http://www.berkshire hathaway.com/letters/2009ltr.pdf. This development demonstrates the success of GEICO's growth strategy. As the late Bruce Henderson noted, "Any really useful strategy must include a means of upsetting the competitive equilibrium and re-establishing it again on a more favorable basis." *Henderson on Corporate Strategy*, 3.

Appendix 9.1. Note on Estimating Growth Value

This appendix contains material from the *Journal of Private Equity*, © 2011 by Institutional Investor, which is reprinted with permission. The author would like to thank James E. Schrager for helpful questions, comments, and suggestions on earlier drafts of this appendix. Any error or omission is solely my fault.

1. Benjamin Graham, David Dodd, and Sidney Cottle, *Security Analysis*, 4th ed. (New York: McGraw-Hill, 1962), 508–509.

2. Robert Hagstrom, *The Warren Buffett Way*, 3rd ed. (Hoboken, NJ: Wiley, 2014), 67.

3. These authors use return on capital (*RoC*) and capital (*C*) in the derivation of their equations (Bruce Greenwald, et al., *Value Investing: From Graham to Buffett and Beyond* [New York: Wiley, 2001], 138–145). As these terms were not defined, I changed them to *RNAV* and *EPV* based, in part, on my notes from Columbia University's value investing class; specifically, Bruce Greenwald, *Value Investing Lecture 4 Mimeo*, Columbia Business School (2002).

4. Greenwald, et al., *Value Investing*, 143.

5. Greenwald, et al. were correct when they observed, "The trouble is that value estimates based on this kind of growth are likely to be highly unreliable in practice" (145). To explain, consider Jim Grant's thoughts on Benjamin Graham's reaction to John Burr Williams, *Theory of Investment Value* (Boston, MA: Harvard, 2002 [1938]):

> The rub, as he [Benjamin Graham] pointed out, was that, in order to apply Williams' method, one needed to make some very large assumptions about the future course of interest rates, the growth of profit, and the terminal value of the shares when growth stops. "One wonders," Graham mused, "whether there may not be too great a discrepancy between the necessarily hit-or-miss character of these assumptions and the highly refined mathematical treatment to which they are subjected.

> Source: James Grant, "Benjamin Graham and *Security Analysis*: The Historical Backdrop," in Benjamin Graham and David Dodd, *Security Analysis*, 6th ed. (New York: McGraw-Hill, 2009), 18.

6. "Miscalculation and misfortune, as much as anything, were responsible for IMM's [International Mercantile Marine's] failure. Morgan and the company's promoters misjudged the gains to be derived from the anticipated growth in trans-Atlantic traffic." Vincent Carosso, *The Morgans: Private International Bankers 1854–1913* (Cambridge, MA: Harvard, 1987), 492. According to Morgan biographer Jean Strouse, "The shipping trust [as the IMM was sometimes referred to] had been a financial fiasco for years. Now it was a human catastrophe as well." *Morgan: American Financier* (New York: Random House, 1999), 643.

7. Calandro, chapter 4 in *Applied Value Investing* (New York: McGraw-Hill, 2009).

10. Value Realization at GTI Corporation

This chapter contains material from *Strategy & Leadership*, © 2007 by Emerald Publishing, which is reprinted with permission. The author would like to thank Edward I. Altman for helpful questions, comments, and suggestions on earlier drafts of this chapter. Any errors or omissions are solely my fault.

1. Rodney Klein, ed., *Benjamin Graham on Investing: Enduring Lessons from the Father of Value Investing* (New York: McGraw-Hill, 2009), 390.

2. Howard Marks, *The Most Important Thing: Uncommon Sense for the Thoughtful Investor* (New York: Columbia University Press, 2011), 11.

3. On the importance of acting contrary to the crowd in a value investing context see Joseph Calandro, Jr., *Value Investing General Principles*, September 21, 2016, available at SSRN: https://ssrn.com/abstract =2575429.

4. For one example, see Johnny Hopkins, "Seth A. Klarman: Successful Value Investing Requires a Multi-Strategy Approach," *The Acquirer's Multiple*, May 7, 2018, https://acquirersmultiple.com/2018/05/seth-klarman -successful-value-investing-requires-a-multi-strategy-approach/.

5. For an example see Nicholas Dunbar, *The Devil's Derivatives: The Untold Story of the Slick Traders and Hapless Regulators Who Almost Blew Up Wall Street . . . and Are Ready to Do It Again* (Boston, MA: Harvard Business School Press, 2011), 173, 264n19.

6. Roger Lowenstein, *When Genius Failed: The Rise and Fall of Long-Term Capital Management* (New York: Random House, 2000), 234–235. See also Nassim Nicholas Taleb, *Fooled by Randomness: The Hidden Role of Chance in Life and in the Markets*, 2nd ed. (New York: Random House, 2005 [2004]), 241–244.

7. Robert Carton and Charles Hofer, *Measuring Organizational Performance: Metrics for Entrepreneurship and Strategic Management Research* (Northampton, MA: Edward Elgar, 2006). Statistically, for the three-year high/low sample (with a size of 120 and timeframe of January 1, 1999–December 31, 2002), the variability explained by the change in Altman's Z-score was .59 (Adjusted R^2), which was higher than the study's other measures and is statistically significant (p-value less than .01; p. 176). In practical language, the change in Z-score provides substantial information about market-adjusted returns for firms similar to those included in the study. Note that those firms did not include financial services firms (135).

8. For information on the practical use of analytics in a professional sports setting see Michael Lewis, *Moneyball: The Art of Winning an Unfair Game* (New York: Norton, 2003); Tom Verducci, *The Cubs Way: The Zen of Building the Best Team in Baseball and Breaking the Curse* (New York: Crown, 2017); and Ben Reiter, *Astroball: The New Way to Win It All* (New York: Crown, 2018).

9. Edward I. Altman, "Financial Ratios, Discriminate Analysis and the Prediction of Corporate Bankruptcy," *Journal of Finance* (September 1968): 589–609.

10. See, for example, Edward I. Altman and Edith Hotchkiss, *Corporate Financial Distress and Bankruptcy: Predict and Avoid Bankruptcy, Analyze and Invest in Distressed Debt*, 3rd ed. (Hoboken, NJ: Wiley, 2006).

11. Edward I. Altman, ed., *Bankruptcy & Distressed Restructurings: Analytical Issues and Investment Opportunities* (Washington, DC: Beard, 1999). For information on distressed investing see Martin J. Whitman and Fernando Diz, *Distress Investing: Principles and Technique* (Hoboken, NJ: Wiley, 2009).

12. Robert S. Kaplan and David P. Norton, "The Balanced Scorecard," *Harvard Business Review*, January–February 1992: 76.

13. Carton and Hofer, *Measuring Organizational Performance*, 78–79, 94.

14. This section is based on Edward I. Altman and James La Fleur, "Managing a Return to Financial Health," *Journal of Business Strategy*, Summer 1981: 31–38, and Michael Ball, "Z Factor: Rescue by the Numbers," *Inc. Magazine*, December 1980: 45–48.

15. Altman and La Fleur, "Managing a Return to Financial Health," 32. As of mid-2018, the accuracy rate has been estimated between 80 and 90 percent.

16. With the three-year high/low sample (with a size of 120 and time-frame of January 1, 1999–December 31, 2002), the variability explained by the growth rate of operating cash flow was only .02 (Adjusted R^2), which was far lower than the variability explained by the change in Z-score. These results were not as statistically significant (p-value less than .10) as those described above. Carton and Hofer, *Measuring Organizational Performance*, 176.

17. Ball, "Z Factor," 46.

18. Altman and La Fleur, "Managing a Return to Financial Health," 36.

19. Altman and La Fleur, "Managing a Return to Financial Health," 34, 36.

20. Altman and La Fleur, "Managing a Return to Financial Health," 37; the growth calculation is mine and has been rounded.

11. Value Realization at the Union Pacific

This chapter contains material from *Financial History*, © 2016 by the Museum of American Finance, which is reprinted with permission. The author would like to thank Maury Klein for coauthoring the paper that preceded this chapter. Any errors or omissions are solely my fault.

1. Jason Zweig and Rodney Sullivan, ed., *Benjamin Graham: Building a Profession* (New York: McGraw-Hill, 2010), 79.

2. Maury Klein, *Union Pacific: The Birth of a Railroad 1862–1893* (New York: Doubleday, 1987), 400.

3. As an example, compare and contrast the profile of the "Erie War," in Norton Reamer and Jesse Downing, *Investment: A History* (New York: Columbia, 2016), 177–179, with that of Maury Klein, *The Life and Legend of Jay Gould* (Baltimore, MD: Hopkins, 1986), 79–87.
More sophisticated critics recognize "that as a finance capitalist, Gould was ahead of his time, that his rivals despised him primarily because he beat them at their own game." However, they go on to claim that "Gould also made a mockery of a supposedly self-regulating capitalist system." Both quotes are from Joshua Wolff, *Western Union and Creation of the American Corporate Order, 1845–1893* (New York: Cambridge, 2013), 261. Significantly, the U.S. financial system has *never* been "self-regulating" to the extent that term implies the absence of governmental participation and/or intervention. It is very important to understand this.
Interestingly, misconceptions of Gould even extend to expert financial historians such as Edward Chancellor, *Devil Take the Hindmost: A History of Financial Speculation* (NY: Farrar, Straus and Giroux, 1999), 173 (footnote †), which references Matthew Josephson's famous work *The Robber Barons* and his comments on Gould, which have been successfully refuted by Klein, *The Life and Legend of Jay Gould*, 495–497.

4. Maury Klein, "In Search of Jay Gould," *Business History Review* 52, no. 2 (Summer 1978): 195.

5. The data source is William Goetzmann, Roger Ibbotson, and Liang Peng, "A New Historical Database for the NYSE 1815 to 1925: Performance and Predictability," *Journal of Financial Markets* 4 (2001): 29. The calculation is mine and has been rounded.

6. On the length of this depression/recession see the National Bureau of Economic Research, http://www.nber.org/cycles.html. For more information on the Panic of 1873 see M. John Lubetkin, *Jay Cooke's Gamble: The*

Northern Pacific Railroad, The Sioux, and the Panic of 1873 (Norman: University of Oklahoma Press, 2006).

7. According to Marc Faber, "The deflationary epoch that followed the global crisis of 1873 was also poor for asset holders . . . many sectors experienced massive bankruptcies and poor business conditions—for example, canals and railroads in the U.S. from 1873 to 1895." *The Gloom, Boom & Doom Report*, December 1, 2018: 6, 8. Significantly, President Ulysses S. Grant refused to sign Bill S. 617, which was known as the "inflation bill." Suffice it to say, the economy went on to recover. Modern politicians and economists of both parties, take note! For more information see Ronald White, *American Ulysses: A Life of Ulysses S. Grant* (New York: Random House, 2016), 545–547.

8. This profile is drawn from Klein, *The Life and Legend of Jay Gould*, which is a book that I very much recommend.

9. For example, "stock manipulation by firms engaged in canal and railroad construction was one of the oldest money-making dodges in the United States." David Lavender, *The Great Persuader: A Major Biography of the Greatest of All the Railroad Moguls* (New York: Doubleday, 1970), 166.

10. For information on Collis Huntington, see Lavender, *The Great Persuader*.

11. Klein, *The Life and Legend of Jay Gould*, 490.

12. For information on Cornelius Vanderbilt see T. J. Stiles, *The First Tycoon: The Epic Life of Cornelius Vanderbilt* (New York: Knopf, 2009).

13. Thus, in the 1880s, the UP was the government's largest debtor. For more information see James Grant, *Mr. Speaker! The Life and Times of Thomas B. Reed, the Man Who Broke the Filibuster* (New York: Simon & Schuster, 2011), 245.

14. Thomas Cochran observed, "Getting out of Erie in a strong cash position on the eve of the panic of 1873, [Gould] was ready to attack the Union Pacific." Klein, *The Life and Legend of Jay Gould*, 137.

15. Maury Klein, *Union Pacific: The Birth of a Railroad 1862–1893* (New York: Doubleday, 1987), 314.

16. Klein, *Union Pacific*, 312–313. "It is the genius of financiers and lawyers alike to transform the simplest of propositions into a labyrinth and profit from the bewildered groping that follows." Klein, *The Life and Legend of Jay Gould*, 51. Jay Gould was "a master architect of labyrinths" as are many of today's successful professional value investors.

17. Martin J. Whitman and Fernando Diz, *Modern Security Analysis: Understanding Wall Street Fundamentals* (Hoboken, NJ: Wiley, 2013), 404.

18. According to Klein, *Union Pacific*, Jay Gould "provided the Union Pacific with its first taste of effective, cohesive management by giving closer attention to every aspect of its operations than any previous officer had done" (311–312).

19. Klein, *Union Pacific*, 309.

20. Klein, *The Life and Legend of Jay Gould*, 154–157.

21. Klein, *The Life and Legend of Jay Gould*, 147.

22. Eric Beinhocker, *The Origin of Wealth: Evolution, Complexity, and the Radical Remaking of Economics* (Boston, MA: Harvard, 2006), 332. See also **Chapter 5** of this book.

23. We are excluding from this list strategies that profit from misplaced governmental rules and regulations. Such strategies led, for example, to the tax shelter frauds of the 1980s (Kurt Eichenwald, *Serpent on the Rock* [New York: Harper, 1995]), the Savings and Loan crisis (Martin Mayer, *The Greatest-Ever Bank Robbery: The Collapse of the Savings and Loan Industry* [New York: Scribner, 1990]), and the financial engineering escapades that triggered, among other things, the 2007–2008 financial crisis (Frank Partnoy, *Infectious Greed: How Deceit and Risk Corrupted the Financial Markets* [New York: Times Books, 2003]).

24. James Grant, "Musk, Edison, Tesla," *Grant's Interest Rate Observer* 34, no. 17 (September 16, 2015): 4.

25. Return on investment (ROI) often serves as a proxy for total return, which may or may not be appropriate for certain investments.

26. For more information see, for example, Steven L. Mintz, *Five Eminent Contrarians: Careers, Perspectives and Investment Tactics* (Burlington, VT: Fraser, 1994), ix–xiv. Jay Gould "spent much of his time and energy swimming against the tide." Klein, *The Life and Legend of Jay Gould*, 196.

27. Humphrey Neill, *The Art of Contrary Thinking*, 5th and Enlarged Ed. (Caldwell, ID: Caxton, 1992 [1954]), 1. See also Mintz, *Five Eminent Contrarians*, ix.

28. James Grant, "Read the Footnotes," *Grant's Interest Rate Observer* 32, no. 22 (November 14, 2014): 3.

29. Howard Marks, *The Most Important Thing: Uncommon Sense for the Thoughtful Investor* (New York: Columbia University Press, 2011), 93.

30. Robert Hagstrom, *The Warren Buffet Way*, 3rd ed. (Hoboken, NJ: Wiley, 2014), refers to this phenomenon as "the institutional imperative" (55–57).

31. According to Howard Marks, this "is the tendency that caused John Maynard Keynes to observe, 'Worldly wisdom teaches that it is better for reputation to fail conventionally than to succeed unconventionally'" (foreword in Hagstrom, *The Warren Buffet Way*, xiv). And thus, as value investor Jean-Marie Eveillard insightfully observed, "It is warmer inside the herd; it is terribly lonely to be a [professional] value investor." Maggie Mahar, *Bull!—A History of The Boom, 1982–1999* (New York: HarperBusiness, 2003), 215.

32. Michael Lewis, *Liar's Poker: Rising Through the Wreckage of Wall Street* (New York: Norton, 1989), 175. Note also Mahar, *Bull!*, 225–226.

33. There are significant strategic implications to this behavior. For example, military strategist Sun Tzu said, "Only to see victory when it is already clear to all is by no means the height of excellence; a victory that is acclaimed by all and sundry is by no means the greatest of victories." James Trapp, tr., Sun Tzu, *The Art of War* (New York: Chartwell, 2012), 25. Similarly, Benjamin Graham observed in *The Intelligent Investor*, 4th ed. (New York: Harper & Row, 1973): "If it is true that a fairly large segment of the stock market is often discriminated against or entirely neglected in the standard analytical selection, then the intelligent investor may be in a position to profit from the resultant undervaluation" (204).

34. Janet Lowe, ed., *The Rediscovered Benjamin Graham: Selected Writings of the Wall Street Legend* (New York: Wiley, 1999), 275.

35. Joseph Calandro, Jr., "Taking Burlington Northern Railroad Private," *Journal of Private Equity* 13, no. 4 (Fall 2010): 8–16.

36. Alice Schroeder, "Buffett Revisits Hunting Ground for Survivors," *Bloomberg*, November 4, 2009.

37. *Berkshire Hathaway Annual Report, 2010,* http://www.berkshire hathaway.com/2010ar/2010ar.pdf.

38. This was an insight that drove Michael Milken. For more information see Robert Sobel, chapters 4–11, in *Dangerous Dreamers: The Financial Innovators from Charles Merrill to Michael Milken* (New York: Wiley, 1993).

39. According to Klein, *The Life and Legend of Jay Gould,* Gould "understood the principle of never moving one piece in isolation from the others" (186).

40. Philip A. Fischer, *Common Stocks and Uncommon Profit and Other Writings* (Hoboken, NJ: Wiley, 2003 [1996]), 241.

41. Klein, *Union Pacific,* 309. Similar comments have been made about the legendary information theorist Claude Shannon: "Importantly, his courage was joined to an ego so self-contained and self-sufficient that it looked, from certain angles, like the absence of ego. This was the keystone quality of Shannon, the one that enabled all the others." Jimmy Soni and Rob Goodman, *A Mind at Play: How Claude Shannon Invented the Information Age* (New York: Simon & Schuster, 2017), 278. Significantly, Shannon was a friend of Henry Singleton, an investor in Teledyne (**Chapter 5**) and one of its board members.

42. See, for example, John P. Hussman, "Debt-Financed Buybacks Have Quietly Placed Investors on Margin," *Hussman Funds Market Comment,* August 17, 2017, https://www.hussmanfunds.com/wmc/wmc150817.htm.

43. According to James Grant, "All Together Now, Buy Stock," *Grant's Interest Rate Observer* 32, no. 5 (March 7, 2018): 1:

We humans seem genetically incapable of buying low and selling high. The other way around suits us better, especially when we sit in serious ponderation around corporate conference tables. According to FactSet, the average price at which the companies of the S&P 500 repurchased stock between the fourth quarter of 2012 and the third quarter of 2013 was 99.8 percent of the average price for the preceding 12 months. In other words, managements bought in shares not because the price was low, or the value commanding. They bought in shares, as we read the managerial mind, because everyone else was buying them.

44. S. L. Mintz, "Working on the Railroad," *Institutional Investor* (May 2006), 27. Mintz is the coauthor of the late value investor John Neff's autobiography, *John Neff on Investing* (New York: Wiley, 1999), which I highly recommend.

Conclusion and Information Advantage

1. Benjamin Graham, *The Memoirs of the Dean of Wall Street* (New York: McGraw-Hill, 1996), 315.

2. Note the example in the **Appendix** to this book's **Introduction**.

3. James Nisbet, *The Entrepreneur* (Charlotte, NC: Capital Technology, Inc., 1976), and George Roberts and Robert McVicker, *Distant Force: A Memoir of the Teledyne Corporation and the Man Who Created It* (self-published, 2007).

4. "What does information really measure? It measures the uncertainty we overcome. . . . We can turn unfair odds to our favor." Jimmy Soni and Rob Goodman, *A Mind at Play: How Claude Shannon Invented the Information Age* (New York: Simon & Schuster, 2017), 142–144. As noted above, Claude Shannon was a friend and classmate of Henry Singleton's, as well as a long-term investor in, and board member of, Teledyne. Shannon's investment in Teledyne compounded at a rate of 27 percent over twenty-five years (239).

5. Benjamin Graham observed in *The Intelligent Investor*, 4th ed. (New York: Harper & Row, 1973): "But if it is true that a fairly large segment of the stock market is often discriminated against or entirely neglected in the standard analytical selections, then the intelligent investor may be in a position to profit from the resultant undervaluations" (204).

6. For more information see Tom Verducci, *The Cubs Way: The Zen of Building The Best Team in Baseball and Breaking the Curse* (New York: Crown, 2017).

7. Ben Reiter, *Astroball: The New Way to Win It All* (New York: Crown, 2018), 227.

8. See, for example, Keith Law, *Smart Baseball: The Story Behind the Old Stats That Are Ruining the Game, the New Ones That Are Running It, and the Right Way to Think About Baseball* (New York: Meadow Party, 2017).

9. "Everyone wants to be [a contrarian], but no one is, for the sad reason that most investors [and corporate managers] are scared of looking foolish. [They] do not fear losing money as much as they fear solitude, by which I mean taking risks that others avoid. When they are caught losing money alone, they have no excuse for their mistake, and most investors [and corporate managers], like most people, need excuses." Michael Lewis, *Liar's Poker* (New York: Norton, 1989), 175.

10. Ted Seides, "What Billy Beane and Jim Simons Have in Common: Investors Clamor for Transparency—But Sometimes, a Lack of It Works to Their Advantage," *Institutional Investor*, September 28, 2018, https://www.institutionalinvestor.com/article/b1b4x0pmqyhnc2/What-Billy-Beane-and-Jim-Simons-Have-in-Common?.

11. Kathleen Elkins, "Warren Buffett's Partner Charlie Munger Says There Are '3 Rules for a Career,'" *CNBC*, August 17, 2017, https://www.cnbc.com/2017/08/16/warren-buffetts-partner-charlie-munger-has-3-rules-for-a-career.html.

12. And we need more George C. Marshalls in government. He was described by George Kennan as "the American gentleman at his best—honorable, courteous, devoid of arrogance, exacting of others but even more of himself." Daniel Kurtz-Phelan, *The China Mission: George Marshall's Unfinished War, 1945–1947* (New York: Norton, 2018), 357.

13. Referencing rather than quoting from Robert Sutton, *The No Asshole Rule: Building a Civilized Workplace and Surviving One That Isn't* (New York: Warner Business, 2010).

Index